family
food

family food

Kay Scarlett

LAUREL
GLEN

San Diego, California

Contents

Breakfast

Scrambled eggs and salmon on brioche

4 fresh eggs
4 tablespoons cream
2 tablespoons unsalted butter
4½ oz. smoked salmon, sliced
2 teaspoons finely chopped dill
2 individual brioche or croissants

Crack the eggs into a bowl, add the cream, and beat well together. Season with some salt and freshly ground black pepper.

Melt the butter in a nonstick frying pan. When it starts to sizzle, add the eggs and turn the heat down to low. Using a flat-ended wooden spoon, push the mixture around until it starts to set, then add the salmon and dill. Continue to cook, gently folding the salmon and dill through the mixture until the eggs are mostly cooked and just a little liquid is left in the pan.

Cut the top off the brioche or croissants, scoop out some of the filling, then pile the scrambled eggs on top and serve.

Serves 2

Savory breakfast tarts

1³/₄ cups all-purpose flour
½ cup plus 2 tablespoons butter,
    diced
9 eggs
4 slices ham
2 tablespoons chopped parsley
2 medium tomatoes, finely chopped
½ cup cream
4 tablespoons grated Parmesan
    cheese

Preheat the oven to 400°F. Sift the flour and ½ teaspoon salt into a food processor, add the butter, and process for a few seconds until the mixture resembles bread crumbs. Bring the dough together using your hands and shape into a ball. Wrap the ball in plastic wrap, flatten slightly, and put in the fridge for 10 minutes.

Roll the pastry out on a floured work surface until it is very thin. Cut out four 6½-in. circles and use them to line four 4-in. tart pans. Press the pastry gently into the flutes of the pans. Line each pan with a piece of crumpled baking parchment and some uncooked rice. Bake for 5 minutes, then take out the parchment and rice and bake for another minute.

Line each tart bottom with the ham (you may need to cut it into pieces to make it fit neatly). Sprinkle with the parsley and add the tomatoes. Gently break two eggs into each pan, then pour a quarter of the cream over the top of each, sprinkle with Parmesan, and dust with salt and pepper.

Put the tarts in the oven and bake for 10–12 minutes or until the egg whites are set. Serve hot or cold.

Serves 4

Cheese and onion waffles with herbed ricotta and roast tomatoes

4 Roma tomatoes, halved
1 tablespoon olive oil
1 tablespoon balsamic vinegar
1 teaspoon sugar
1 tablespoon chopped oregano
1¼ cups low-fat ricotta cheese
4 tablespoons chopped herbs
  (oregano, sage, rosemary, parsley)
1½ cups self-rising flour
3 tablespoons freshly grated
  Parmesan cheese
3 tablespoons grated low-fat
  cheddar cheese
3 large scallions, finely chopped
1 egg
1 cup low-fat milk
2 egg whites
fresh oregano sprigs, to garnish

Preheat the oven to 315°F. Lightly grease a baking tray. Place the tomato halves on the tray and drizzle the cut surface with olive oil and balsamic vinegar. Sprinkle with the sugar, oregano, and salt. Bake for 1 hour or until very soft. Put the ricotta in a bowl and fold in the chopped herbs. Season to taste. Divide the herbed ricotta mixture into four even portions. Refrigerate until needed.

Meanwhile, place the flour, Parmesan, cheddar, scallions, whole egg, and milk in a bowl. Season with salt and black pepper, then mix well. Whisk the egg whites until soft peaks form, then gently fold into the cheese and egg mixture.

Preheat a waffle iron and brush lightly with olive oil. Pour in ⅓ cup waffle batter and cook until golden on both sides. Keep warm in the oven while you cook the remaining waffles.

To serve, arrange the waffle halves on each serving plate with two tomato halves and some herbed ricotta mixture on the side. Garnish with a sprig of fresh oregano.

Serves 4

French toast with crispy prosciutto

3 tablespoons light cream or milk
3 eggs
3 tablespoons superfine sugar
pinch of cinnamon
about ⅓ cup butter
8 thick slices bread, cut in half
　diagonally
1 tablespoon olive oil
12 slices prosciutto

Put the cream, eggs, sugar, and cinnamon in a wide, shallow bowl and mix together. Soak the bread in the egg mixture, one slice at a time, shaking off any excess.

Melt half the butter in a frying pan. When it is sizzling, add three or four slices of bread in a single layer and cook until golden brown on both sides. Cook the remaining bread in batches, adding more butter as needed, and keeping the cooked slices warm in the oven until all are done.

Next, in a separate frying pan, heat the olive oil. When hot, add the prosciutto and fry until crisp. Remove and drain on paper towels. Place the prosciutto on top of the French toast and serve.

Serves 4

Fried eggs and tomatoes on scallion potato cakes

Scallion potato cakes
10½ oz. potatoes, peeled and roughly
   chopped
1 egg yolk
½ cup grated cheddar cheese
3 scallions, trimmed and finely
   chopped
2 tablespoons finely chopped Italian
   parsley
1 tablespoon all-purpose flour
2 tablespoons olive oil

2 tablespoons olive oil, extra
1 garlic clove, sliced
3 Roma tomatoes, halved lengthwise
butter, for frying
4 eggs

Boil the potatoes in a saucepan of salted water until tender. Drain, then return the potatoes to the pan over low heat to dry. Remove the pan from the heat and mash the potatoes. Stir in the egg yolk, cheese, scallions, and parsley and season. Form into four patties. Place the flour on a plate and lightly coat the patties. Cover and chill for 30 minutes.

Heat the olive oil in a large frying pan over medium heat. Fry the patties for 4–5 minutes on each side until golden brown. Keep warm until needed.

In a separate frying pan, heat the extra olive oil over low heat. Add the garlic and fry for 2 minutes. Add the tomatoes cut-side down and fry for 10–15 minutes, turning them once during cooking.

Heat a heavy-bottomed, nonstick frying pan over medium heat and add 2 tablespoons oil and a little butter. When the butter is sizzling, break the eggs into the frying pan. Cook for about 1 minute. Turn off the heat and leave to stand for 1 minute. Serve the eggs with the potato cakes and tomatoes.

Serves 2

Eggs Benedict

12 eggs, cold
8 slices prosciutto
4 English muffins, split
1 cup butter
2 tablespoons lemon juice

Preheat the broiler. Put a large frying pan full of water over high heat. When the water is bubbling, turn the heat down to a simmer. Crack an egg into a cup and slip the egg into the water. The egg should start to turn opaque as it hits the water. Do the same with seven more eggs, keeping them separated. Turn the heat down and let the eggs cook for 3 minutes.

Put the prosciutto on a baking sheet, place it under the broiler for 2 minutes, then turn it over and cook the other side. Put the muffins in a toaster or under the broiler to toast.

Crack the remaining four eggs into a blender and put the lid on, leaving the top hole open. Heat the butter in a small pan until it has melted.

Start the blender and pour in the butter in a steady stream. The eggs should thicken immediately to make a thick sauce. Add the lemon juice and season with salt and black pepper.

Put the muffins on plates and put a slice of prosciutto on each. Lift each egg out of the water, drain, and put on top of the prosciutto. Spoon some of the hollandaise sauce over each egg.

Serves 4

Broiled mushrooms with garlic and chili

4 large or 8 medium mushrooms
2 tablespoons butter, softened
1 garlic clove, crushed
1–2 small red chilies, finely chopped
4 tablespoons finely chopped parsley
4 thick slices ciabatta
tomato chutney or relish
crème fraîche, to serve

Turn on the broiler and cover the broiler pan with a piece of foil so any juices stay with the mushrooms as they cook. Gently pull the stems out of the mushrooms and peel the caps.

Mix together the butter, garlic, chili, and parsley and spread some over the inside of each mushroom. Make sure the butter is quite soft so it spreads easily. Season well.

Broil the mushrooms under a medium heat for about 8 minutes to cook thoroughly. Test the centers with the point of a knife if you are not sure.

Toast the bread, spread some tomato chutney or relish on each slice, then top with a mushroom or two and serve with a dollop of crème fraîche.

Serves 4

Piperade

2 tablespoons olive oil
1 large onion, thinly sliced
2 red bell peppers, seeded and
  julienned
2 garlic cloves, crushed
5 medium tomatoes
pinch of cayenne pepper
8 eggs, lightly beaten
1 tablespoon butter
4 thin slices of mild smoked ham

Heat the oil in a large, heavy-based frying pan over medium heat, then add the onion. Cook for about 3 minutes or until soft. Add the red pepper and garlic, cover, and cook for 8 minutes, stirring frequently to ensure the mixture doesn't brown.

Cut a cross in the bottom of each tomato. Put in a large bowl of boiling water for 20 seconds, then drain and plunge into a bowl of cold water. Remove the tomatoes and peel the skin away from the cross. Chop the flesh and discard the cores. Add the chopped tomato and cayenne to the red pepper mixture, cover the pan, and cook for another 5 minutes.

Uncover the pan and increase the heat. Cook for 3 minutes or until the juices have evaporated, shaking the pan often. Season well with salt and freshly ground black pepper. Add the eggs and scramble into the mixture until fully cooked.

Heat the butter in a small frying pan over medium heat and fry the ham. Arrange the piperade on four plates, then top with the cooked ham. Serve with buttered toast.

Serves 4

Mushroom omelette with chorizo

3$\frac{1}{2}$ tablespoons butter
1 medium chorizo sausage, sliced
1 cup mushrooms, finely sliced
6 eggs
2 tablespoons chives, finely chopped

Heat 2 tablespoons of the butter in a small omelette pan or frying pan over medium heat. Add the chorizo and fry for about 5 minutes or until golden. Remove from the pan using a slotted spoon. Add the mushrooms to the pan and cook, stirring frequently, for about 4 minutes or until soft. Add to the chorizo.

Break the eggs into a bowl and season with salt and freshly ground black pepper. Add the chives and beat lightly with a fork.

Put half the remaining butter in the pan and melt over medium heat until foaming. Add half the eggs and cook for 20 seconds, until they start to set on the bottom, then quickly stir the mixture with a fork. Work quickly, drawing away some of the cooked egg from the bottom of the pan and allowing some of the uncooked egg to set, tilting the pan a little as you go. Once the eggs are mostly set, arrange half the mushrooms and chorizo on top. Cook for 1 minute more, if necessary. Slide the omelette onto a plate and keep warm while the second omelette is cooking. Repeat with the remaining ingredients. Serve as soon as both omelettes are cooked.

Serves 2

Croque madame

3 eggs
1 tablespoon milk
1 1/2 tablespoons butter, softened
4 slices good-quality white bread
1 teaspoon Dijon mustard
4 slices Gruyère cheese
2 slices ham
2 teaspoons vegetable oil

Crack 1 egg into a wide, shallow bowl, add the milk, and lightly beat. Season with salt and freshly ground black pepper.

Butter the bread using 1/2 tablespoon of the butter, then spread half the slices with Dijon mustard. Place a slice of cheese on the slices with mustard, then the ham, and then another slice of cheese. Top with the remaining bread.

Heat the remaining butter and vegetable oil in a large nonstick frying pan over medium heat. While the butter is melting, dip one sandwich into the egg and milk mixture, coating the bread on both sides. When the butter is sizzling, add the sandwich and cook for 1 1/2 minutes on one side, pressing down firmly with a spatula. Turn over and cook the other side, then move it to the side of the pan.

Gently break an egg into the pan and fry until it is done to your taste. Transfer the sandwich to a plate and top with the fried egg. Keep warm while you repeat with the remaining sandwich and egg, adding more butter and oil to the pan if necessary. Serve immediately.

Makes 2 sandwiches

Cheese and herb cornbread with scrambled eggs

Cornbread
1 1/4 cups self-rising flour
1 tablespoon superfine sugar
2 teaspoons baking powder
1 teaspoon salt
3/4 cup fine polenta
1/2 cup grated cheddar cheese
1/2 cup chopped mixed herbs (chives,
   dill, parsley)
2 eggs
1 cup buttermilk
1/3 cup macadamia or olive oil

Scrambled eggs
6 eggs
1/2 cup cream
small basil leaves, to garnish

Preheat the oven to 350°F. Grease an 8 x 4-in. loaf pan. Sift the flour, sugar, baking powder, and salt into a bowl. Add the polenta, cheddar, herbs, eggs, buttermilk, and oil and mix to combine. Spoon the mixture into the loaf pan and bake for 45 minutes or until a skewer inserted into the center comes out clean. Remove from the pan.

To make the scrambled eggs, whisk together the eggs and cream and season with salt and pepper. Pour the mixture into a nonstick frying pan and cook over low heat, stirring occasionally, until the egg is just set. (The more you stir the eggs, the more scrambled they become.) Serve the scrambled eggs with slices of buttered cornbread. Sprinkle with basil leaves.

Serves 4

Huevos rancheros

1 ½ tablespoons olive oil
1 white onion, finely chopped
1 green bell pepper, finely chopped
2 red chilies, finely chopped
1 garlic clove, crushed
½ teaspoon dried oregano
2 tomatoes, chopped
2 (14-oz.) cans chopped tomatoes
8 eggs
4 flour tortillas
⅔ cup feta cheese, crumbled

Put the olive oil in a large frying pan over a medium heat. Add the onion and green pepper and fry them gently together for 3 minutes or until they are soft.

Add the chilies and garlic and stir briefly, then add the oregano, fresh and canned tomatoes, and ¾ cup water. Bring to a boil, then turn down the heat, cover with a lid, and simmer gently for 8–10 minutes or until the sauce thickens. Season with salt and pepper.

Smooth the surface of the mixture, then make eight hollows with the back of a spoon. Break an egg into each hollow and cover the pan. Cook the eggs for 5 minutes or until they are set.

While the eggs are cooking, heat the tortillas according to the instructions on the package and cut each into quarters.

Serve the eggs with some feta crumbled over them and the tortillas on the side.

Serves 4

Banana bread

3 ripe bananas, well mashed
2 eggs, well beaten
2 teaspoons grated orange zest
2 cups all-purpose flour
1 teaspoon ground cinnamon
1 teaspoon salt
1 teaspoon baking soda
$3/4$ cup superfine sugar
$1/2$ cup walnuts, coarsely chopped

Preheat the oven to 350ºF. Grease a 8 x 4-in. loaf pan.

Combine the bananas, eggs, and orange zest in a large bowl. Sift in the flour, cinnamon, salt, and baking soda, mix, then add the sugar and walnuts. Mix thoroughly, then pour into the prepared pan. Bake for 1 hour 10 minutes or until a skewer inserted into the center comes out clean.

Serve warm or allow to cool, then toast and serve buttered.

Makes 1 loaf

Creamed rice with minted citrus compote

3/4 cup basmati rice
2 cups milk
4 cardamom pods, bruised
1/2 cinnamon stick
1 clove
3 tablespoons honey
1 teaspoon natural vanilla extract

Minted citrus compote
2 red grapefruit, peeled and
   segmented
2 oranges, peeled and segmented
3 tablespoons orange juice
1 teaspoon grated lime zest
3 tablespoons honey
8 fresh mint leaves, finely chopped

Cook the rice in a large saucepan of boiling water for 12 minutes, stirring occasionally. Drain and cool.

Place the rice, milk, cardamom pods, cinnamon stick, and clove in a saucepan and bring to a boil. Reduce the heat to low and simmer for 15 minutes, stirring occasionally, until the milk is absorbed and the rice is creamy. Remove the spices, then stir in the honey and vanilla.

To make the compote, combine the grapefruit, orange, orange juice, lime zest, honey, and mint and mix until the honey has dissolved. Serve with the rice.

Serves 4

Cinnamon oatmeal with caramel figs and cream

2 cups rolled oats
1/4 teaspoon ground cinnamon
3 1/2 tablespoons butter
1/2 cup brown sugar
1 1/4 cups cream
6 fresh figs, halved
milk, to serve
heavy cream, to serve

Place the oats, 4 cups water, and the cinnamon in a saucepan and stir over a medium heat for 5 minutes or until the oatmeal becomes thick and smooth. Set aside.

Melt the butter in a large frying pan, add all but 2 tablespoons of the brown sugar, and stir until it dissolves. Stir in the cream and bring to a boil, then simmer for 5 minutes or until the sauce starts to thicken slightly.

Place the figs on a baking tray, sprinkle with the remaining sugar, and broil until the sugar is melted.

Spoon the oatmeal into individual bowls, top with a little milk, then divide the figs and the caramel sauce among the bowls. Top each serving with a large dollop of cream.

Serves 4

Healthy nut and seed granola

8 cups puffed corn cereal
1 1/2 cups rolled oats
1 cup pecans
1 cup macadamia nuts, roughly
  chopped
1 1/4 cups flaked coconut
1 cup flaxseed, sunflower, and
  almond mix or other seed-nut mix
1/2 cup dried apples, chopped
1/2 cup dried apricots, chopped
1 1/4 cups dried pears, chopped
1/2 cup maple syrup
1 teaspoon vanilla extract

Preheat the oven to 350°F. Place the puffed corn, rolled oats, pecans, macadamia nuts, coconut, seed-nut mix, apples, apricots, and pears in a bowl and mix to combine.

Place the maple syrup and vanilla in a small saucepan and cook over low heat for 3 minutes or until the maple syrup becomes easy to pour. Pour the maple syrup over the mixture and toss lightly to coat.

Divide the granola mixture between two nonstick baking trays. Bake for about 20 minutes, turning frequently, until lightly toasted. Allow to cool before transferring it to an airtight container.

Makes 2 1/4 pounds granola

Blueberry pancakes

1 cup buttermilk
1 egg, lightly beaten
1 tablespoon melted butter
1 teaspoon vanilla extract
$3/4$ cup all-purpose flour
1 teaspoon baking powder
$1/2$ teaspoon salt
2 ripe bananas, mashed
$1/2$ cup blueberries
1 teaspoon vegetable oil
maple syrup, to serve

Put the buttermilk, egg, butter, and vanilla in a bowl and whisk together. Sift in the flour, baking powder, and salt, then stir, making sure not to overblend, as the batter should be lumpy. Add the fruit.

Heat the oil in a frying pan over medium heat. Add $1/4$ cup of batter to the pan for each pancake. Cook for 3 minutes or until the pancakes are golden brown on the bottom. Turn over and cook for another minute. Repeat with the rest of the batter, keeping the cooked pancakes warm. Serve immediately, drizzled with maple syrup.

Makes about 12 pancakes

Broiled fruit with cinnamon toast

2 tablespoons low-fat margarine
1 1/2 teaspoons ground cinnamon
4 thick slices good-quality brioche
4 ripe plums, halved and pits removed
4 ripe nectarines, halved and pits
  removed
2 tablespoons honey

Place the margarine and 1 teaspoon of the cinnamon in a bowl and mix until well combined. Broil the brioche on one side until golden. Spread the other side with half the cinnamon spread, then grill until golden. Keep warm in the oven.

Brush the plums and nectarines with the remaining spread and broil until the spread is bubbling and the fruit is lightly browned at the edges.

To serve, place two plum halves and two nectarine halves on each toasted slice of brioche. Dust with the remaining cinnamon and drizzle with the honey.

Serves 4

Note: Canned plums or apricots may be used in place of fresh fruit.

Raspberry breakfast crepes

2 cups all-purpose flour
pinch of salt
1 teaspoon sugar
2 eggs, lightly beaten
2 cups milk
1 tablespoon butter, melted
3$\frac{1}{3}$ cups raspberries
confectioners' sugar, for dusting
maple syrup or honey, to serve

Sift the flour, salt, and sugar into a bowl and make a well in the center. In a bowl, mix the eggs and milk together with $\frac{3}{8}$ cup water. Slowly pour the mixture into the well, whisking all the time to incorporate the flour and create a smooth batter. Stir in the melted butter. Cover and refrigerate for 20 minutes.

Heat a crepe pan or a small nonstick frying pan over medium heat and lightly grease. Pour in enough batter to coat the base of the pan in a thin, even layer. Pour off any excess. Cook for 1 minute or until the crepe starts to come away from the side of the pan. Turn over and cook on the other side for 1 minute more until just golden. Repeat the process, stacking the crepes on a plate with baking parchment between them and covered with foil, until all the batter is used up.

To serve, put one crepe on a serving plate. Arrange some raspberries on a quarter of the crepe. Fold the crepe in half, then in half again, so that the raspberries are wrapped in a little triangular pocket. Repeat with the remaining crepes and raspberries. Dust with confectioners' sugar, drizzle with maple syrup or honey, and serve.

Makes 8 large crepes

Mixed berry couscous

1 cup couscous
2 cups apple and cranberry juice
1 cinnamon stick
1 cup raspberries
1 cup blueberries
1 cup blackberries
1 cup strawberries, halved
zest of 1 lime
zest of 1 orange
scant 1 cup plain yogurt
2 tablespoons light corn syrup
mint leaves, to garnish

Place the couscous in a bowl. Place the apple and cranberry juice in a saucepan with the cinnamon stick. Bring to a boil, then remove from the heat and pour over the couscous. Cover with plastic wrap and allow to stand for 5 minutes or until all the liquid has been absorbed. Remove and discard the cinnamon stick.

Separate the grains of the couscous with a fork, add the raspberries, blueberries, blackberries, strawberries, lime zest, and orange zest, and fold in gently. Spoon the mixture into four bowls and serve with a generous dollop of yogurt and a drizzle of light corn syrup. Garnish with mint leaves.

Serves 4

Ginger and ricotta pancakes with fresh honeycomb

1 cup whole-wheat flour
2 teaspoons baking powder
2 teaspoons ground ginger
2 tablespoons superfine sugar
1 cup flaked coconut, toasted
4 eggs, separated
2 cups ricotta cheese
1¼ cups milk
4 bananas, sliced
7 oz. fresh honeycomb, broken into large pieces

Sift the flour, baking powder, ginger, and sugar into a bowl. Stir in the coconut and make a well in the center. Add the combined egg yolks, 1½ cups of the ricotta, and all of the milk. Mix until smooth.

Beat the egg whites until soft peaks form, then fold into the pancake mixture.

Heat a frying pan over low heat and brush lightly with a little melted butter or oil. Pour ¼ cup of the batter into the pan and swirl gently to create an even pancake. Cook until bubbles form on the surface. Flip and cook the other side for 1 minute or until golden. Repeat until all the batter is used up.

Stack three pancakes onto each plate and top with a generous dollop of ricotta, sliced bananas, and a large piece of fresh honeycomb.

Serves 4

Lunch

Thai chicken sausage rolls

1 lb. 2 oz. ground chicken
1 teaspoon ground cumin
1 teaspoon ground coriander
2 tablespoons sweet chili sauce
2 tablespoons chopped cilantro
  leaves
1 cup fresh bread crumbs
2 sheets frozen puff pastry, thawed
1 egg, lightly beaten
1 tablespoon sesame seeds
arugula leaves, to serve
sweet chili sauce, extra, for dipping

Preheat the oven to 400°F. Combine the chicken, cumin, coriander, chili sauce, coriander, and bread crumbs in a bowl.

Spread the mixture along one edge of each pastry sheet and roll up to conceal the filling. Place the rolls seam-side down on a baking pan lined with baking parchment, brush lightly with the beaten egg, and sprinkle with sesame seeds. Bake for 30 minutes or until golden and cooked through. Slice the rolls and serve with arugula and sweet chili sauce.

Serves 6–8

Fattoush with fried haloumi

2 cucumbers
4 pita breads
1 garlic clove, crushed
2 tablespoons lemon juice
5 tablespoons olive oil
4 scallions, sliced
4 tomatoes, diced
2 green bell peppers, diced
1 bunch Italian parsley, chopped
2 tablespoons mint, chopped
2 tablespoons oregano, chopped
sumac (optional)
2 lb. 4 oz. haloumi cheese, cut
  into 8 slices

Preheat the broiler. Peel the cucumber, cut it into quarters lengthwise, then cut each piece into thick slices. Place in a sieve and sprinkle with a little salt to help drain off any excess liquid.

Split each pita bread in half and toast on both sides to crisp. When the bread is crisp, break it into small pieces. Mix the garlic, lemon juice, and 4 tablespoons of the oil to make a dressing. Rinse and drain the cucumber.

Put the cucumber, scallions, tomatoes, green peppers, parsley, mint, and oregano in a large bowl. Add the dressing and toss everything together well.

Heat the last tablespoon of oil in a nonstick frying pan and fry the haloumi cheese on both sides until it is browned. Sprinkle the bread over the salad and fold it through.

Serve the fattoush with the slices of haloumi on top. Sprinkle with a little sumac if desired.

Serves 4

Spanish omelette with smoked salmon

1 tablespoon olive oil
3 medium potatoes, peeled and
  cubed
1 onion, finely chopped
8 eggs
2 tablespoons dill, chopped
8 slices smoked salmon
1/3 cup mascarpone cheese
4 handfuls salad leaves

Heat the oil in a nonstick frying pan and add the potato cubes. Fry them gently, stirring them so they brown on all sides and cook through to the middle. This should take about 10 minutes. Cut a cube open to see if it is cooked through completely.

When the potatoes are cooked, add the onion and cook it gently for a few minutes until it is translucent and soft. Preheat the broiler.

When the onion is almost ready, break the eggs into a bowl and whisk them together with some salt and freshly ground pepper and the dill.

Tear the smoked salmon into pieces and add it to the frying pan. Add the mascarpone in dollops. Using a spatula, pull the mixture into the center of the pan and smooth over. Pour the eggs over the top and cook for 5–10 minutes or until the omelette is just set.

Put the frying pan under the broiler for a minute or two to lightly brown the top of the omelette. Slide the omelette out of the frying pan and cut it into eight wedges. Arrange a handful of salad leaves on each plate and top with two wedges of omelette.

Serves 4

Bagels with smoked salmon and caper salsa

4 plain or rye bagels
7 tablespoons cream cheese
7 oz. sliced smoked salmon
2 scallions, chopped
2 Roma tomatoes, finely chopped
2 tablespoons small capers
2 tablespoons finely chopped
  fresh dill
2 tablespoons lemon juice
1 tablespoon extra-virgin olive oil

Cut the bagels in half and spread the bottom half generously with cream cheese, then top with the salmon.

Combine the scallions, tomatoes, capers, dill, lemon juice, and olive oil in a bowl. Pile this mixture onto the salmon and serve.

Serves 4

Wild rice salad

½ cup wild rice
1 cup chicken stock
1 tablespoon butter
½ cup basmati rice
2 slices bacon, chopped and cooked
¾ cup currants
½ cup slivered almonds, toasted
1 cup chopped parsley
6 scallions, finely sliced
grated zest and juice of 1 lemon
olive oil, to drizzle
lemon wedges, to serve

Put the wild rice and stock in a saucepan, add the butter, bring to a boil, then cook, covered, over low heat for 1 hour. Drain.

Put the basmati rice in a separate saucepan with cold water and bring to a boil. Cook at a simmer for 12 minutes, then drain. Mix with the cooked wild rice and cool.

Combine the rice with the bacon, currants, almonds, parsley, scallions, and lemon zest and juice. Season, drizzle with olive oil, and serve with lemon wedges.

Serves 4

Tomato caponata with mozzarella

2 small eggplants, cubed
olive oil, for frying
1 onion, cubed
2 celery stalks, sliced
1 red bell pepper, cubed
4 ripe Roma tomatoes, chopped
9 oz. red cherry tomatoes, halved
9 oz. yellow cherry tomatoes, halved
2 tablespoons red wine vinegar
1/4 teaspoon sugar
2 tablespoons capers, rinsed
1/2 cup unpitted black olives
4 cups shredded mozzarella cheese
large handful of parsley, roughly
    chopped

Cook the eggplant in boiling salted water for 1 minute, then drain. Squeeze out any excess moisture with your hands.

Heat 2 tablespoons of olive oil in a large frying pan and add the eggplant. Brown on all sides over high heat, adding more oil if needed. When the eggplant is cooked, drain it on paper towels.

Add a little more oil to the pan, turn down the heat, and cook the onion and celery for about 5 minutes, until soft but not brown. Add the red pepper and cook it for 2 minutes. Add the chopped Roma tomatoes and a couple of tablespoons water. Simmer the mixture for 5 minutes, or until the mixture is quite dry, then stir in the cherry tomatoes.

Season the mixture well with black pepper. Add the red wine vinegar, sugar, capers, and olives and cook for 4–5 minutes over low heat. Add the drained eggplant and cook for 5–10 minutes. Take the mixture off the heat and leave it to cool. Toss the mozzarella and parsley through the caponata and serve with a green salad and some bread to mop up the juices.

Serves 4

Creamy egg salad

10 large eggs, plus 1 egg yolk
3 teaspoons lemon juice
2 teaspoons Dijon mustard
1/3 cup olive oil
1/3 cup safflower oil
2 tablespoons chopped dill
2 tablespoons crème fraîche or
  sour cream
2 tablespoons capers, rinsed and
  drained
1/3 cup young mustard greens or
  watercress

Put the whole eggs in a saucepan of water. Bring to a boil and simmer for 10 minutes. Drain, then cool under cold water and peel.

To make the dressing, place the egg yolk, lemon juice, and Dijon mustard in a food processor and season. With the motor running, slowly add the oils, drop by drop, increasing to a thin, steady stream as the mixture thickens. When combined, put the mayonnaise in a large bowl, add the dill, crème fraîche or sour cream, and capers.

Chop the eggs and add to the mayonnaise. Put in a serving bowl, sprinkle over just the tips of the greens, and serve.

Serves 4

Tomato and pesto bruschetta

8 thick slices ciabatta
1/3 cup olive oil
1/2 cup pesto
8 ripe Roma tomatoes
1/3 cup mascarpone cheese

Preheat the broiler. To make the bruschetta, brush both sides of each piece of bread with olive oil and put the bread on a baking sheet. Grill for 3 minutes on each side or until crisp and golden brown.

Spread a teaspoon of pesto over each piece of bruschetta and remove from the sheet. Slice the tomatoes into four pieces lengthwise and drain them for a minute on a piece of paper towel—this will keep the juice from the tomatoes from making the bruschetta soggy. Put the tomato slices on the baking sheet.

Broil the tomatoes for 5 minutes, by which time they will start to cook and brown at the edges. When the tomatoes are cooked, layer four slices onto each piece of bruschetta. Put the bruschetta back on the sheet and broil it for another minute to heat through. Add a dollop of mascarpone and a little more pesto to each bruschetta and serve hot.

Serves 4

Grilled asparagus with salsa

3 eggs
2 tablespoons milk
1 tablespoon olive oil
2 ears corn
1 small red onion, diced
1 red bell pepper, finely chopped
2 tablespoons chopped fresh thyme
2 tablespoons olive oil, extra
2 tablespoons balsamic vinegar
24 fresh asparagus spears
1 tablespoon macadamia oil
toasted whole-wheat bread, to serve

Beat the eggs and milk to combine. Heat the oil in a nonstick frying pan, add the egg, and cook over a medium heat until just set. Flip and cook the other side. Remove and allow to cool, then roll up and cut into thick slices.

Cook the corn on a grill or in boiling water until tender. Set aside to cool slightly, then slice off the corn kernels. Make the salsa by gently combining the corn, onion, red pepper, thyme, olive oil, and balsamic vinegar.

Trim off any woody ends from the asparagus, lightly brush with macadamia oil, and cook on the grill until tender. Serve the asparagus topped with a little salsa and the finely shredded egg, accompanied by fingers of buttered, toasted whole-wheat bread.

Serves 4–6

Fried egg and red onion wrap

1 ½ tablespoons olive oil
3 red onions, thickly sliced
1 large red bell pepper, sliced
3 tablespoons balsamic vinegar
4 eggs
4 lavash breads
4 tablespoons sour cream
sweet chili sauce

Heat the olive oil in a nonstick frying pan and add the onion. Cook it slowly, stirring occasionally until it softens and turns translucent. Add the red pepper and continue cooking until both the onion and pepper are soft. Turn up the heat and stir for a minute or two, until they start to brown, then stir in the balsamic vinegar. Remove the mixture from the pan and keep warm.

Carefully break the eggs into the frying pan, keeping them separate if you can. Cook over a gentle heat until the eggs are just set.

Heat the lavash breads under the broiler or in a microwave for a few seconds (you want them to be soft and warm). Lay the breads out on a board, spread a tablespoon of sour cream onto the center of each, then drizzle with a little chili sauce. Put a heap of the onion and pepper mixture on each and top with an egg. Season with salt and pepper.

Fold in one short end of each piece of lavash bread and then roll each one up lengthwise.

Serves 4

Mediterranean BLT

4 small vine-ripened tomatoes, halved
1 head garlic, halved
1 tablespoon extra-virgin olive oil
¼ cup basil leaves
1 loaf Italian bread
8 slices provolone cheese
8 slices mortadella
1 bunch arugula
extra-virgin olive oil, extra
balsamic vinegar

Preheat the oven to 400°F. Place the tomatoes and garlic in a roasting pan and drizzle with the oil. Sprinkle with salt and cracked black pepper and roast for 40 minutes or until the garlic is soft and the tomatoes are slightly dried. Add the basil leaves and continue cooking for 5 minutes or until the leaves are crisp. Remove from the oven.

Cut four thick slices from the loaf of bread and lightly toast on both sides. Peel the roasted garlic cloves and spread half onto the toast. Top with the provolone, mortadella, arugula, basil, and roasted tomatoes. Sprinkle with the remaining roasted garlic, drizzle with extra olive oil and the balsamic vinegar, and serve immediately.

Serves 4

Mini sweet potato and leek frittatas

2 lb. 4 oz. orange sweet potatoes
  (about 6 medium)
1 tablespoon olive oil
2 tablespoons butter
4 leeks, white part only, thinly sliced
2 garlic cloves, crushed
1 2/3 cups feta cheese, crumbled
8 eggs
1/2 cup cream

Preheat the oven to 350°F. Grease twelve 1/2-cup muffin tins. Cut small rounds of baking parchment and place in the base of each. Cut the sweet potatoes into small cubes and boil, steam, or microwave until tender. Drain well and set aside.

Heat the oil and butter in a large frying pan, add the leek, and cook for about 10 minutes, stirring occasionally, until very soft and lightly golden. Add the garlic and cook for 1 minute more. Cool, then stir in the feta and sweet potatoes. Divide the mixture evenly among the muffin tins.

Whisk the eggs and cream together and season with salt and freshly ground black pepper. Pour the egg mixture into each tin until three-quarters filled, then press the vegetables down gently. Bake for 25–30 minutes or until golden and set. Leave in the tins for 5 minutes, then ease out with a knife and cool on a wire rack before serving.

Makes 12

Thai chicken with glass noodles

4 tablespoons coconut cream
1 tablespoon fish sauce
1 tablespoon brown sugar
2 chicken breasts, skinned and
  cut into shreds
4½ oz. glass noodles
2 stems lemongrass
4 kaffir lime leaves
1 red onion, finely chopped
large handful of cilantro leaves,
  chopped
large handful of mint, chopped
1–2 red chilies, sliced
3 green bird's-eye chilies, finely sliced
2 tablespoons roasted peanuts,
  chopped
1–2 limes, cut in halves or quarters

Mix the coconut cream in a small saucepan or a wok with the fish sauce and brown sugar and bring to a boil, then add the chicken and simmer until the chicken is cooked through. This should only take a minute if you stir it a couple of times. Leave the chicken to cool in the sauce. Soak the noodles in boiling water for a minute or two—they should be translucent and soft when they are ready. Drain them, then, using a pair of scissors, cut them into shorter lengths.

Peel the lemongrass until you reach the first purplish ring, then trim off the root. Make two or three cuts down through the bulblike root, finely slice across it until it starts to get harder, then throw the hard top piece away. Pull the stems out of the lime leaves by folding the leaves in half, with the shiny side inward, and pulling down on the stalk. Roll up the leaves tightly, then slice them very finely across.

Put all the ingredients, except the lime, in a bowl with the noodles and chicken, with its sauce, and toss. Squeeze the lime pieces over the dish and toss again.

Serves 4

Steak baguette with arugula and mustardy mayo

3 tablespoons olive oil, plus extra
  for frying
1 red onion, sliced
1 teaspoon brown sugar
2 teaspoons balsamic vinegar
1 teaspoon thyme
1 tablespoon Dijon mustard
3 tablespoons mayonnaise
1 1/2 cups arugula
1 lb. 2 oz. tenderloin steak, cut into
  4 thin slices
2 thick baguettes, cut in half, or
  8 thick slices of good-quality bread
2 tomatoes, sliced

Heat 2 tablespoons oil in a small saucepan. Add the onion and cook very slowly, with the lid on, stirring occasionally, until the onion is soft but not brown, up to 15 minutes. Remove the lid, add the sugar and vinegar, and cook for another 10 minutes or until the onion is soft and just browned. Take the pan off the stove and stir in the thyme.

Meanwhile, make the mustardy mayo by mixing together the mustard and mayonnaise in a small bowl.

Drizzle the arugula leaves with the remaining olive oil and season with salt and freshly ground black pepper.

Heat 1 tablespoon of the extra oil in a frying pan over high heat and cook the steaks for 2 minutes on each side, adding more oil if necessary. Season to taste.

To serve, put out the bread, along with separate bowls containing the onion, mustardy mayo, arugula, steak, and sliced tomatoes. Let everyone make their own baguette so they can get the perfect mix of all the flavors.

Serves 4

Grilled baby octopus

4 lb. 8 oz. baby octopus
1½ cups red wine
3 tablespoons balsamic vinegar
2 tablespoons soy sauce
½ cup sweet chili sauce
1 cup Thai basil leaves, to serve

Clean the octopus, taking care not to break the ink sacs. Place the octopus, red wine, and balsamic vinegar in a large, nonaluminum saucepan and bring to a boil. Reduce the heat and simmer for 15 minutes or until just tender. Drain and transfer to a bowl. Add the soy sauce and sweet chili sauce.

Heat a barbecue grill to high and cook the octopus until it is sticky and slightly charred. Serve on a bed of Thai basil leaves.

Serves 4

Beef salad with sweet-and-sour cucumber

2 cucumbers
4 teaspoons superfine sugar
1/3 cup red wine vinegar
1 tablespoon vegetable oil
2 large or 4 small fillet steaks, cut into strips
8 scallions, cut into pieces
2 garlic cloves, crushed
2 tablespoons ginger, grated
2 tablespoons soy sauce
4 handfuls mixed lettuce leaves

Halve the cucumber lengthwise, then slice thinly and put in a colander. Sprinkle with a little bit of salt and leave for about 10 minutes. This will draw out any excess moisture.

Meanwhile, put 2 teaspoons each of the sugar and the vinegar in a bowl and stir until the sugar dissolves. Rinse the salt, then drain the cucumber very thoroughly before patting it with a paper towel to soak up any leftover moisture. Mix the cucumber with the vinegar mixture.

Heat half the oil in a frying pan until it is smoking. Add half the steak and fry for a minute. Remove from the pan and repeat with the remaining oil and steak. Return to the same pan, then add the scallions and fry for another minute. Add the garlic and ginger, toss, then add the soy sauce and remaining sugar and vinegar. Cook until the sauce turns sticky, then quickly remove from the heat.

Put a handful of lettuce leaves on four plates and divide the beef among them. Sprinkle some cucumber on the beef and serve the rest on the side.

Serves 4

Individual herbed lemon ricotta

2¼ cups ricotta cheese

Dressing
2 tablespoons olive oil
1 garlic clove, crushed
zest of 1 lemon
2 tablespoons lemon juice
1 tablespoon balsamic vinegar
½ cup olive oil
1 cup sun-dried tomatoes, roughly
   chopped
4 tablespoons parsley, chopped

crusty bread, to serve

Lightly grease and line four ½-cup ramekins with plastic wrap. Divide the ricotta among them, and press down firmly. Cover with plastic wrap and refrigerate for 2 hours.

Preheat the oven to 425°F. Unmold each ricotta onto a tray lined with baking parchment and bake for 20 minutes or until golden.

To make the dressing, combine all the ingredients in a bowl. Place the ricottas on a serving platter. Spoon a little of the dressing around each one, drizzling a little over the top.

Serves 4

Caesar salad

1½ heads romaine lettuce
16 thin baguette slices
1¼ cups olive oil
6 slices bacon, chopped
1 egg yolk
1 garlic clove
4 anchovy fillets
1 tablespoon lemon juice
Worcestershire sauce, to taste
chunk of Parmesan cheese

Tear the lettuce into pieces and put in a large bowl. Preheat the broiler.

Brush the baguette slices on both sides with some of the oil and broil until they are golden brown all over. Leave to cool.

Fry the bacon in a little oil until it browns, then sprinkle it over the bowl of lettuce.

Put the egg yolk, garlic, and anchovies in a blender and whizz for a minute, then, with the motor still running, add the remaining oil in a steady stream. The oil and egg should thicken immediately and form mayonnaise. Add the lemon juice and Worcestershire sauce, stir well, and season with salt and pepper.

Using a potato peeler, make some Parmesan curls by running the peeler along one edge of the cheese. Try to make the curls as thin as possible.

Pour the dressing over the lettuce, add the Parmesan curls, and toss everything together well. Divide the salad among four bowls and arrange the slices of toasted baguette on each one.

Serves 4

Barbecued sweet chili seafood on banana mats

1 lb. 2 oz. shrimp, peeled and
  deveined, tails left intact
10½ oz. scallops
1 lb. 2 oz. calamari, cleaned and
  hoods cut in quarters
1 lb. 2 oz. baby octopus, cleaned
1 cup sweet chili sauce
1 tablespoon fish sauce
2 tablespoons lime juice
3 tablespoons peanut oil
banana leaves, cut into squares,
  to serve
lime wedges, to serve

Place the shrimp, scallops, calamari, and octopus in a shallow, nonmetallic bowl.

In a separate bowl, combine the sweet chili sauce, fish sauce, lime juice, and 1 tablespoon of the peanut oil. Pour the mixture over the seafood and mix gently to coat. Allow to marinate for 1 hour. Drain the seafood well and reserve the marinade.

Heat the remaining oil in a grill pan. Cook the seafood in batches over high heat for 3–5 minutes or until tender. Drizzle each batch with a little of the leftover marinade during cooking.

Pile the seafood high onto the squares of banana leaf and serve with wedges of lime if desired.

Serves 4

Spinach and zucchini frittata

1 tablespoon olive oil
1 red onion, thinly sliced
2 zucchini, sliced
1 garlic clove, crushed
10½ oz. spinach leaves, stalks
   removed
6 eggs
2 tablespoons cream
3 oz. Swiss cheese, grated

Heat the oil in a medium nonstick frying pan and fry the onion and zucchini over medium heat until they are a pale golden brown. Add the garlic and cook it for a minute. Add the spinach and cook until the spinach has wilted and any excess moisture has evaporated—if you don't do this, your frittata will end up soggy in the middle, as the liquid will continue to come out as it cooks. Shake the pan so you get an even layer of mixture. Turn the heat to low.

Beat the eggs and cream together and season with salt and pepper. Stir in half of the cheese and pour the mixture over the spinach. Cook the bottom of the frittata for about 4 minutes or until the egg is just set. While you are doing this, preheat the broiler. When the bottom of the frittata is set, sprinkle the rest of the cheese on top and put the frying pan under the broiler to cook the top.

Turn the frittata out of the frying pan after leaving it to set for a minute. Cut into wedges to serve.

Serves 4

Mushrooms with marinated feta

2 large tomatoes
20 fresh asparagus spears
10½ oz. marinated feta cheese, sliced
¼ cup extra-virgin olive oil
zest of 1 lemon
2 garlic cloves, crushed
2 tablespoons lemon juice
4 large mushrooms, brushed clean
  and stems removed
4 eggs
fresh oregano, to garnish

Cut the tomatoes into thick slices.
Trim the ends from the asparagus.

Drain the oil from the feta and place
into a nonmetallic bowl. Stir in the
olive oil, lemon zest, garlic, and lemon
juice. Season with cracked black
pepper.

Place the mushrooms and tomatoes
in a shallow dish and pour the oil
mixture over them. Toss gently to
coat, and marinate for 15 minutes.
Drain the mushrooms, reserving the
marinade, and cook them, together
with the tomatoes, on a lightly oiled
barbecue grill plate until tender.

Add the asparagus toward the end of
cooking, and then the eggs. Place the
mushrooms on a plate, top each one
with some asparagus spears, a slice
of tomato, an egg, and some sliced
feta. Drizzle with the marinade and
garnish with oregano.

Serves 4

Grilled cheese, aioli, and ham sandwich

1 loaf ciabatta
1 garlic clove, crushed
$1/2$ cup mayonnaise
4 slices ham
$2/3$ cup sun-dried tomatoes, chopped
2 tablespoons capers, chopped
6–8 slices cheddar cheese

Preheat the broiler. Cut the bread in half horizontally and then into four equal pieces. Toast all the pieces. To make the aioli, mix the garlic into the mayonnaise and season it well with salt and pepper.

Spread the aioli over each slice of bread. Put a slice of ham on four of the pieces and then divide the sun-dried tomatoes and capers among them. Top with enough cheese slices to make a good layer, then put them on a baking sheet.

Grill the sandwiches until the cheese melts and starts to bubble, then put the top slices back on and press down firmly.

Cut each sandwich in half diagonally and enjoy.

Serves 4

Steak sandwiches with salsa verde

2 garlic cloves, crushed
4 handfuls parsley
1/2 bunch basil leaves
1/2 bunch mint leaves
3 tablespoons olive oil
2 teaspoons capers, chopped
2 teaspoons lemon juice
2 teaspoons red wine vinegar
4 minute steaks
4 large pieces ciabatta, halved
   horizontally
1 cucumber, sliced

To make the salsa verde, put the garlic and herbs in a food processor with 2 tablespoons of the oil and process until they are coarsely chopped. Place the chopped herbs into a bowl and stir in the capers, lemon juice, and vinegar. Season with salt and pepper.

Heat the remaining oil in a frying pan and fry the steaks for 1 minute on each side—they should cook very quickly and start to brown.

While the steaks are cooking, toast the bread. Spread some salsa verde on all the pieces of the bread and make four sandwiches with the steaks and cucumber.

Serves 4

Pizzette

1 cup all-purpose flour
1 cup whole-wheat flour
2 teaspoons dry yeast
1/2 teaspoon sugar
1/2 teaspoon salt
2 tablespoons plain yogurt
2 tablespoons tomato paste
1 garlic clove, crushed
1 teaspoon dried oregano
1/2 oz. sliced ham
2 teaspoons grated mozzarella
  cheese
chopped arugula leaves, to serve
extra-virgin olive oil, to serve

Sift the all-purpose flour into a bowl, then add the whole-wheat flour, dry yeast, sugar, and salt. Make a well in the center, add 1/2 cup water and the yogurt, and mix to a dough. Knead on a lightly floured surface for 5 minutes or until smooth and elastic. Cover with a towel and rest in a warm place for 20–30 minutes or until doubled in size.

Preheat the oven to 400°F. Punch the dough down and knead for 30 seconds, then divide into four portions. Roll each portion into a 6-in. round and place on a baking sheet.

Combine the tomato paste, garlic, oregano, and 1 tablespoon water. Spread the paste over each crust, then top with the ham and mozzarella. Bake for 12–15 minutes or until crisp and golden on the edges. Just before serving, top with chopped arugula and drizzle with extra-virgin olive oil.

Makes 4

Salade niçoise

8 small salad potatoes (about 1 lb.
  5 oz.)
1 cup small green beans, trimmed
  and halved
1 tablespoon olive oil
14 oz. tuna steak, cubed
1 garlic clove, crushed
1 teaspoon Dijon mustard
2 tablespoons white wine vinegar
½ cup olive oil, extra
4 handfuls green lettuce leaves
12 cherry tomatoes, halved
½ cup black olives
2 tablespoons capers, drained
4 hard-boiled eggs, cut into wedges
8 anchovies, halved
lemon wedges

Cook the potatoes in boiling salted water for about 10 minutes or until they are just tender. Drain, cut into wedges, then put in a bowl. Cook the beans in boiling salted water for 3 minutes, then drain and hold under cold running water for a minute (this will keep them from cooking any more). Add them to the potatoes.

Heat the olive oil in a frying pan and, when it is hot, cook the tuna cubes for about 3 minutes or until they are browned on all sides. Add these cubes to the potatoes and beans.

Whisk together the garlic, mustard, and vinegar, then add the extra oil in a thin, steady stream, whisking until smooth. Season well.

Cover the base of a large bowl with the lettuce leaves. Sprinkle the potatoes, beans, tuna, tomatoes, olives, and capers over the leaves and drizzle with the dressing. Decorate with the egg wedges and anchovies. Squeeze some lemon juice over the salad.

Serves 4

Bacon and avocado salad

8 slices bacon
1 cup green beans, trimmed and
  halved
10½ oz. spinach leaves
2 shallots, finely sliced
2 avocados
¼ teaspoon brown sugar
1 garlic clove, crushed
⅓ cup olive oil
1 tablespoon balsamic vinegar
1 teaspoon sesame oil

Preheat the broiler. Put the bacon on a baking sheet and cook on both sides until it is nice and crisp. Leave to cool, then break into pieces.

Bring a saucepan of water to a boil and cook the beans for 4 minutes. Drain and then hold them under cold running water for a few seconds to stop them from cooking any further.

Put the spinach in a large bowl and add the beans, bacon, and shallots. Halve the avocados, then cut into cubes and add to the bowl.

Mix the brown sugar and garlic in a small bowl. Add the rest of the ingredients and whisk together to make a dressing.

Pour the dressing over the salad and toss well. Grind black pepper over the top and sprinkle with salt.

Serves 4

Goat cheese, leek, and tapenade parcels

1/2 cup butter
4 leeks, thinly sliced
8 sheets phyllo pastry
2 tablespoons tapenade
4 small thyme sprigs
4 small rounds of goat cheese or
   4 thick slices from a log

Preheat the oven to 350°F. Melt half of the butter in a saucepan, add the leeks, and stir until they are coated in the butter. Cook slowly over low heat until they are completely tender.

Melt the rest of the butter in a small saucepan on the stove. Place one of the sheets of phyllo on the work surface with the short end facing you. Brush the pastry with butter. Lay another sheet right on top of it and cover it with a towel to keep the pastry from drying out. Do the same with the other six sheets.

When the leeks are cooked, uncover the phyllo. Spread a quarter of the tapenade over the middle of each piece of pastry, leaving a wide border around the edges. Divide the leeks among the phyllo, putting them on the tapenade. Top each pile of leek with the goat cheese and then a thyme sprig. Now fold the bottom of the pastry up and the two sides in, to enclose the filling, then fold the top end of the pastry down and roll the whole parcel over. Repeat with the remaining parcels. Brush the pastry with the butter and bake the parcels for 20 minutes. The pastry should be browned and the filling melted.

Serves 4

Spinach salad with chicken and sesame dressing

1 lb. spinach leaves
1 cucumber, peeled and diced
4 scallions, shredded
2 carrots, julienned
2 chicken breasts, cooked
2 tablespoons tahini
2 tablespoons lime juice
3 teaspoons sesame oil
1 teaspoon sugar
pinch of chili flakes
2 tablespoons sesame seeds
large handful of cilantro leaves

Put the spinach in a large bowl. Sprinkle the cucumber, scallions, and carrots over the top. Shred the chicken breast into long pieces and sprinkle it over the vegetables.

Mix together the tahini, lime juice, sesame oil, sugar, and chili flakes, then add salt to taste. Drizzle this dressing over the salad.

Cook the sesame seeds in a dry frying pan over low heat for a minute or two, stirring frequently. When they start to brown and smell toasted, pour them over the salad. Sprinkle the cilantro leaves over the top. Toss the salad just before serving.

Serves 4

Chicken sandwiches

2 skinless chicken breast fillets,
  cut in half horizontally
2 tablespoons olive oil
2 tablespoons lemon juice
4 large pieces ciabatta, cut in half
  horizontally
1 garlic clove, cut in half
mayonnaise
1 avocado, sliced
2 tomatoes, sliced
large handful of arugula leaves, long
  stems snapped off

Flatten each piece of chicken by hitting it either with your fist, the flat side of a knife blade or cleaver, or with a meat mallet. Don't break the flesh, just thin it a bit. Trim off any fat or sinew.

Heat the oil in a frying pan, add the chicken pieces, and fry on both sides for a couple of minutes or until they turn brown and are cooked through (check by cutting into the middle of one). Sprinkle with the lemon juice, then take the chicken out of the pan. Add the bread to the pan with the cut side down and cook for a minute, pressing down on it to flatten it and help soak up any juices. Take the bread out of the pan, rub the cut side of the garlic over the surface, then spread all the pieces with a generous amount of mayonnaise. Put a piece of chicken on four of the pieces, season, then layer with the avocado and tomatoes, seasoning as you go. Finish with the arugula and the tops of the bread, then serve.

Serves 4

Vietnamese chicken salad

2 chicken breasts or 4 chicken thighs,
  cooked
2 tablespoons lime juice
1 1/2 tablespoons fish sauce
1/4 teaspoon sugar
1–2 bird's-eye chilies, finely chopped
1 garlic clove, crushed
2 shallots, finely sliced
2 handfuls bean sprouts
large handful of shredded Chinese
  cabbage
4 tablespoons Vietnamese mint or
  mint leaves, finely chopped

Remove the flesh from the chicken
and shred it. Discard the skin and
bones.

Mix together the lime juice, fish sauce,
sugar, chili, garlic, and shallots.

Bring a saucepan of water to a boil
and throw in the bean sprouts. After
10 seconds, drain and rinse under
cold water to keep them from cooking
any more.

Mix the bean sprouts with the
Chinese cabbage, Vietnamese mint,
and chicken. Pour the dressing over
the salad and toss well.

Serves 4

Barbecued honey chicken wings

12 chicken wings
4 tablespoons soy sauce
3 tablespoons sherry
3 tablespoons vegetable oil
1 garlic clove, crushed
3 tablespoons honey

Rinse the chicken wings, then dry thoroughly by patting with paper towels. Tuck the wing tips in.

Put the chicken wings in a shallow, nonmetallic dish. Whisk together the soy sauce, sherry, oil, and garlic, then pour all over the chicken wings, lightly tossing. Cover with plastic wrap, then place in the fridge for 2 hours to give the chicken a chance to take up some of the marinade—it will help if you turn the wings occasionally.

The honey needs to be heated enough for it to become brushing consistency—either use the microwave or warm it gently in a small saucepan.

Lightly grease a barbecue or grill pan and heat it up. Lift the chicken out of the marinade and add it to the hot pan. Cook the chicken wings until tender and cooked through, turning occasionally, about 12 minutes. Now brush the wings with the warmed honey and cook for 2 more minutes.

Serves 4

Bean enchiladas

1 tablespoon light olive oil
1 onion, finely sliced
3 garlic cloves, crushed
1 bird's-eye chili, finely chopped
2 teaspoons ground cumin
1/2 cup vegetable stock
3 tomatoes, peeled, seeded, and
   chopped
1 tablespoon tomato paste
2 (15-oz.) cans mixed beans
2 tablespoons chopped cilantro
   leaves
8 flour tortillas
1 small avocado, peeled and
   chopped
1/2 cup light sour cream
1/2 cup cilantro sprigs
2 cups shredded lettuce

Heat the oil in a deep frying pan over medium heat. Add the onion and cook for 3–4 minutes or until just soft. Add the garlic and chili and cook for another 30 seconds. Add the cumin, vegetable stock, tomato, and tomato paste and cook for 6–8 minutes or until the mixture is quite thick and pulpy. Season with salt and freshly ground black pepper.

Preheat the oven to 325°F. Drain and rinse the beans. Add the beans to the sauce and cook for 5 minutes to heat through, then add the chopped cilantro.

Meanwhile, wrap the tortillas in foil and warm in the oven for 3–4 minutes.

Place a tortilla on a plate and spread with 1/4 cup of the bean mixture. Top with some avocado, sour cream, cilantro sprigs, and lettuce. Roll the enchiladas up, tucking in the ends. Cut each one in half to serve.

Serves 4

Steamed rice noodle rolls

1 lb. 9 oz. barbecued or roast duck
8 rice noodle rolls
2 scallions, finely shredded
2 thick slices fresh ginger, finely
  shredded
handful of cilantro leaves
oyster sauce, for drizzling
chili sauce, to serve

Cut the duck into bite-sized pieces.
You may have to strip the flesh off the
bones first, depending on how you
bought it—leave the skin on but trim
off any fatty parts.

Gently unroll the rice noodle rolls.
If they are a bit stiff, steam or
microwave them for a minute or two.
If they are in a vacuum-wrapped
package, you can also drop the
wrapped package in boiling water
for 5 minutes.

Put a pile of duck (an eighth of the
whole amount) at one edge of the
narrower end of one noodle roll and
arrange some scallions, ginger, and
cilantro over it. Drizzle with about a
teaspoon of oyster sauce and roll
the sheet up. Repeat this with the
remaining sheets. Put the sheets on
a heatproof plate.

Put the plate in a bamboo or metal
steamer and set the steamer above
a saucepan filled with simmering
water. Put the lid on and steam
for 5 minutes.

Serve the rolls cut into lengths with
some more oyster sauce drizzled
over them and some chili sauce on
the side.

Serves 4

Shrimp mango salad

Dressing
2 tablespoons sour cream
6-oz. can mango puree
3 tablespoons lime juice
1 tablespoon sweet chili sauce

6 slices bacon, chopped
4 lb. 8 oz. cooked jumbo shrimp,
    peeled and deveined, tails intact
3 large mangoes, peeled and cut
    into thin wedges
2 large avocados, sliced

To make the dressing, combine all the
ingredients in a small bowl and whisk
until smooth.

Fry the bacon until crisp, then drain
on paper towels.

Arrange the shrimp, mango, and
avocado on a large platter, then
sprinkle with the bacon bits. Drizzle
with the dressing, then serve.

Serves 6

Spiced parsnip and bacon cake

8 parsnips, cut into pieces
4 tablespoons butter
8 slices bacon, chopped
2 red chilies, finely chopped
4 shallots, finely chopped
1 1/2 teaspoons garam masala
2 tablespoons whole-grain mustard
1 tablespoon honey
1/2 cup cream
green salad, to serve

Bring a saucepan of water to a boil and cook the parsnips at a simmer for 15 minutes. Drain them well.

Melt 2 tablespoons of the butter in a large nonstick frying pan, add the bacon, and cook until browned. Add the chili and chopped shallots and cook for 2 minutes. Stir in the garam masala and remove from the heat.

Mash the parsnips and mix them into the bacon mixture. Put the frying pan back on the heat with the last 2 tablespoons of butter, pile the parsnip mixture into the pan, and flatten it out with a spatula. Cook it for a few minutes—it should hold together in a cake. Loosen the cake, slide it out onto a plate, then invert the plate back over the frying pan and flip the cake back in so you can cook the other side.

While the cake is cooking, mix the mustard, honey, and cream together in a small saucepan over low heat until the mixture bubbles.

When both sides of the cake are brown, turn the cake out onto a board. Cut the cake into wedges and serve with the honey-mustard sauce and a green salad.

Serves 4

Crispy lavash tiles with butter mushrooms

3 pieces lavash or Lebanese bread
2 tablespoons olive oil
1/4 cup finely grated Parmesan cheese
7 tablespoons butter
4 scallions, sliced
1 lb. 10 oz. mixed mushrooms (field, button, cremini, enoki), sliced
1 tablespoon chervil leaves

Preheat the oven to 350°F. Cut the lavash bread into 1 1/4-in.-wide strips and brush lightly with 1 tablespoon of the oil. Sprinkle with the grated Parmesan and bake for 10 minutes or until crispy.

Heat the butter and the remaining oil in a large frying pan until it is sizzling. Add the scallions and the field mushrooms and cook over a medium heat until the mushrooms are tender. Add the button and cremini mushrooms and cook until the liquid has evaporated. Remove from the heat and stir in the enoki mushrooms.

Arrange the toasted strips of lavash bread into an interlocking square. Pile the mushrooms in the center, garnish with chervil, and serve immediately.

Serves 4

Every night

Baked chicken and leek risotto

4 1/2 tablespoons butter
1 leek, thinly sliced
2 chicken breast fillets, cut into
    small cubes
2 cups risotto rice
1/4 cup white wine
5 cups chicken stock
1/3 cup grated Parmesan cheese
2 tablespoons thyme leaves, plus
    extra to garnish
freshly grated Parmesan cheese,
    extra

Preheat the oven to 300°F and put a 5-quart ovenproof dish with a lid in the oven.

Heat the butter in a saucepan over medium heat, stir in the leek, and cook for about 2 minutes, then add the chicken and stir for 3 minutes. Add the rice and stir for 1 minute, then add the wine and stock and bring to a boil.

Pour into the ovenproof dish and cover. Cook in the oven for 30 minutes, stirring halfway through. Remove from the oven and stir in the cheese and thyme. Season, then sprinkle with extra thyme and cheese.

Serves 4

Spaghetti carbonara

1 tablespoon olive oil
10$^1/_2$ oz. pancetta, cut into small dice
$^2/_3$ cup heavy cream
6 egg yolks
14 oz. spaghetti
$^2/_3$ cup grated Parmesan cheese

Heat the olive oil in a saucepan and cook the pancetta, stirring frequently, until it is light brown and crisp. Drain the pancetta of any excess oil.

Mix the cream and egg yolks together in a bowl, and when the pancetta has cooled, add it to the egg mixture.

Cook the spaghetti in a large saucepan of boiling salted water until al dente, stirring once or twice to make sure the pieces are not stuck together. Drain the spaghetti and reserve a small cup of the cooking water.

Put the spaghetti back in the saucepan over low heat. Add the egg mixture and half the Parmesan, then take the pan off the heat, otherwise the egg will scramble. Season with salt and pepper and mix. If the sauce is too thick and the pasta is stuck together, add a little of the reserved cooking water. The spaghetti should look as if it has a fine coating of egg and cream all over it.

Serve the spaghetti in warm bowls with more Parmesan sprinkled over the top.

Serves 4

Minestrone alla Milanese

8 oz. dried cranberry beans
4 tablespoons butter
1 onion, finely chopped
1 garlic clove, finely chopped
3 tablespoons parsley, finely chopped
2 sage leaves
$3\frac{1}{2}$ oz. pancetta, cubed
2 celery stalks, halved, then sliced
2 carrots, sliced
3 potatoes, peeled but left whole
1 teaspoon tomato paste
14-oz. can chopped tomatoes
8 basil leaves
12 cups chicken or vegetable stock
2 zucchini, sliced
8 oz. shelled peas
$\frac{3}{4}$ cup green beans, cut into
   $1\frac{1}{2}$-in. lengths
$\frac{1}{4}$ head of cabbage, shredded
1 cup risotto rice
grated Parmesan cheese, to serve

Put the dried beans in a large bowl, cover with cold water, and soak overnight. Drain and rinse under cold water.

Melt the butter in a saucepan and add the onion, garlic, parsley, sage, and pancetta. Cook over low heat, stirring until the onion is soft.

Add the celery, carrot, and potatoes and cook for 5 minutes. Stir in the tomato paste, tomatoes, basil, and cranberry beans. Season with pepper. Add the stock and bring slowly to a boil. Cover and leave to simmer for 2 hours, stirring once or twice.

If the potatoes have not broken up, roughly break them with a fork against the side of the pan. Taste for seasoning and add the zucchini, peas, green beans, cabbage, and rice. Simmer until the rice is cooked. Serve with the Parmesan cheese.

Serves 6

Tuna mornay

4½ tablespoons butter
2 tablespoons all-purpose flour
2 cups milk
½ teaspoon dry mustard
¾ cup grated cheddar cheese
1 lb. 5 oz. water-packed tuna, drained
2 tablespoons finely chopped parsley
2 hard-boiled eggs, chopped
4 tablespoons fresh bread crumbs
paprika, for dusting

Preheat the oven to 350°F. Melt the butter in a small saucepan, add the flour, and stir over low heat for 1 minute. Take the pan off the heat and slowly pour in the milk, stirring until you have a smooth sauce. Return the pan to the heat and stir constantly until the sauce boils and thickens. Reduce the heat and simmer for another 2 minutes. Remove the pan from the heat and whisk in the mustard and two-thirds of the cheese—don't stop whisking until you have a smooth, rich, cheesy sauce.

Roughly flake the tuna with a fork, then add it to the cheesy sauce along with the parsley and eggs. Season with a little salt and pepper, then spoon the mixture into four 1-cup ovenproof ramekins.

Make the topping by mixing together the bread crumbs and the rest of the cheese, then sprinkle it over the mornay. Add a hint of color by dusting the top very lightly with paprika. Place in the oven until the topping is golden brown, about 20 minutes.

Serves 4

Eggplant parmigiana

3 lb. 5 oz. eggplants
all-purpose flour, seasoned with salt
  and pepper, for coating
1½ cups olive oil
2 cups tomato pasta sauce from a jar
2 tablespoons roughly torn basil
  leaves
2 cups shredded mozzarella cheese
1 cup grated Parmesan cheese

Thinly slice the eggplant lengthwise. Layer the slices in a large colander, sprinkling salt between each layer. Leave for 1 hour to drain. Rinse and pat the slices dry on both sides with paper towels, then coat lightly with the flour.

Preheat the oven to 350°F and grease a shallow 2½-quart baking dish.

Heat ½ cup of the olive oil in a large frying pan. Quickly fry the eggplant slices in batches over high heat until crisp and golden on both sides. Add more olive oil as needed. Drain on paper towels as you remove each batch from the pan.

Make a slightly overlapping layer of eggplant slices over the base of the dish. Season with pepper and a little salt. Spoon 4 tablespoons of pasta sauce over the eggplant and sprinkle some of the basil over the top. Sprinkle with some mozzarella, followed by some Parmesan. Continue layering until you have used all the ingredients, finishing with a layer of the cheeses.

Bake for 30 minutes. Remove from the oven and allow to cool for 30 minutes before serving.

Serves 8

Pizza margherita

2 ready-made pizza crusts or
  2 packages pizza dough
8 very ripe Roma tomatoes
handful of basil leaves
4 garlic cloves, crushed
2 tablespoons tomato paste
5 tablespoons olive oil
4 cups shredded mozzarella cheese

Preheat the oven to its highest setting or according to the instructions on the package of the pizza crust or dough.

Remove the cores, seeds, and juices from the tomatoes, chop the tomatoes roughly, then puree in a food processor with eight basil leaves. Stir in the garlic, tomato paste, and 2 tablespoons of olive oil and season well.

Roll out the pizza dough (if using) to 12-in. circles and put them on oiled baking sheets—if they shrink when you move them, just stretch them out again. Drizzle each with a little olive oil. Spoon the tomato sauce over the dough or crust, spreading it up to the rim. Sprinkle the mozzarella over the top and drizzle with a little more olive oil.

Cook the pizza for 5–12 minutes (or according to the instructions on the package of the pizza crust or dough) or until the base is light brown and crisp and the topping is cooked. Before serving, drizzle with a little more oil and sprinkle the remaining basil over the top.

Makes 2 large pizzas

Mushroom soup

2 tablespoons butter
1 onion, finely chopped
12 large mushrooms, finely chopped
2 garlic cloves, crushed
2 tablespoons dry sherry
4 cups chicken or vegetable stock
2 tablespoons parsley, finely chopped
cream, to taste

Melt the butter in a large saucepan and fry the onion until the onion is translucent but not browned. Add the mushroom and garlic and continue frying. At first the mushrooms will give off a lot of liquid, so keep frying until it is all absorbed. This will take 15–20 minutes.

Add the sherry to the pan, turn up the heat, and let the mixture bubble — this burns off the alcohol but leaves the flavor. Cool slightly, then transfer to a blender. Whizz together until a smooth paste forms, then add the stock and blend until smooth. Add the parsley and a couple of tablespoons of cream and blend together. Pour back into the saucepan and heat gently. Serve with bread.

Serves 4

Shrimp with garlic and chili

½ cup olive oil
6 garlic cloves, crushed
1 red onion, finely chopped
3–4 dried chilies, cut in half, seeds
   removed
32 jumbo shrimp, peeled and
   deveined, tails left intact
4 tomatoes, finely chopped
handful of parsley or cilantro,
   chopped

Heat the oil in a large frying pan or shallow casserole. Add the garlic, onion, and chili, cook for a few minutes, then add the shrimp and cook them for about 4 minutes, by which time they should be pink all over.

When the shrimp are cooked, add the tomatoes and cook for a minute or two. Season with salt and stir in the herbs. Eat with bread to soak up the juices.

Serves 4

Imam bayildi

2 eggplants
5 tablespoons olive oil
2 medium onions, chopped
2 garlic cloves, crushed
6 ripe tomatoes, chopped
1 teaspoon ground cinnamon
large handful of Italian parsley,
  chopped
2 cups tomato juice
plain yogurt, to serve

Preheat the oven to 400°F. Cut the eggplant in half lengthwise. To hollow out the middle, run a small, sharp knife around the edge of each cut half, about 1/2 in. from the skin. Dig out the flesh in the middle, within the cut line, to leave four shells. Keep the flesh and chop it finely.

Heat 4 tablespoons of the oil in a frying pan and fry the eggplant flesh, onion, and garlic until the onion is soft and cooked through. Add the tomatoes and any juices and stir everything together. Season with salt and pepper and add the cinnamon. Cook the mixture until it is mostly dry, then stir in the parsley.

Fill the eggplant shells with the mixture and put them in a large baking dish. Pour the tomato juice around the eggplant—this will help stop the eggplant from drying out as it cooks. Drizzle with the remaining oil.

Bake the eggplant shells for 1 hour and 10 minutes, by which time the flesh should be tender and the filling brown on top. Serve with some of the tomato juice spooned over and a dollop of yogurt on top.

Serves 4

Sausages cooked with lentils

3 tablespoons olive oil
8 Italian sausages
1 onion, chopped
3 garlic cloves, thinly sliced
2 tablespoons finely chopped
  rosemary
18-oz. can tomatoes
16 juniper berries, lightly crushed
1 teaspoon freshly grated nutmeg
1 bay leaf
1 dried chili
scant 1 cup red wine
1/2 cup green lentils
extra rosemary, to garnish

Heat the olive oil in a large saucepan and cook the sausages for 5–10 minutes, browning well all over. Remove the sausages and set aside.

Reduce the heat to low, add the onion and garlic to the pan, and cook until the onion is soft and translucent but not browned. Stir in the rosemary, then add the tomatoes and cook gently until the sauce has thickened.

Add the juniper berries, nutmeg, bay leaf, chili, red wine, and 1 3/4 cups water. Bring to a boil, then add the lentils and the cooked sausages. Stir well, cover the saucepan, and simmer gently for about 40 minutes or until the lentils are soft. Stir the lentils a few times to prevent them from sticking to the bottom of the pan; add a little more water if you need to cook them for a bit longer. Remove the bay leaf and chili before serving. Garnish with rosemary.

Serves 4

Rice noodles with beef, black beans, and peppers

10$\frac{1}{2}$ oz. rump steak
1 garlic clove, crushed
3 tablespoons oyster sauce
2 teaspoons sugar
2 tablespoons soy sauce
5 tablespoons black bean sauce
2 teaspoons cornstarch
$\frac{3}{4}$ teaspoon sesame oil
2 lb. 11 oz. fresh or 1 lb. 5 oz. dried
  flat rice noodles
1$\frac{1}{2}$ tablespoons vegetable oil
2 red bell peppers, sliced
1 green bell pepper, sliced
handful of cilantro leaves

Cut the steak across the grain into thin slices and put it in a bowl with the garlic, oyster sauce, sugar, soy sauce, black bean sauce, cornstarch, and sesame oil. Mix everything together, making sure the slices are well coated.

If you are using dried rice noodles, soak them in boiling water for 10 minutes or until they are opaque and soft. If your noodles are particularly dry, they may need a little longer. Drain the noodles.

Heat the oil in a wok or frying pan and, when it is hot, add the peppers. Stir-fry the peppers for a minute or two until they are starting to soften, then add the meat mixture and cook for a minute. Add the noodles and toss well. Keep cooking until the meat is cooked through and everything is hot, then toss in the cilantro leaves and stir once before turning off the heat. Serve immediately.

Serves 4

Cheesy potato cakes with bacon

4 large or 8 small floury potatoes
  (e.g., russet)
2 tablespoons milk
2 tablespoons butter
1 lb. savoy cabbage, shredded
1 cup shredded cheddar cheese
1 tablespoon vegetable oil
8 slices bacon

Cut the potatoes into pieces and cook them in simmering water for 15 minutes or until they are soft. Drain well, put them back in the pan with the milk, and mash until they are smooth. Season with salt and pepper.

Melt the butter in a nonstick frying pan and cook the cabbage until it is soft. Add this to the potatoes, along with the cheese. The mixture should be stiff enough to form into cakes—it is up to you whether to make large ones or small ones.

Heat the oil in the same frying pan over medium heat and cook the bacon on both sides until it is crisp. Remove the bacon from the pan and keep warm. Add the potato cakes to the pan and fry them on both sides until they are well browned and slightly crisp. Shake the pan occasionally to move the cakes around so they don't stick. Serve with the bacon.

Serves 4

Saffron fish cakes with herb crème fraîche

$^2/_3$ cup milk
2 pinches saffron threads
1 lb. (about 4 medium) white fish fillets
4 large potatoes, cut into chunks
2 garlic cloves, unpeeled
2 tablespoons all-purpose flour
2 teaspoons grated lemon zest
handful of parsley, finely chopped
2 tablespoons cream
$^1/_3$ cup crème fraîche
2 tablespoons mint, finely chopped
2 tablespoons parsley, finely chopped
1–2 tablespoons butter

Put the milk and saffron in a frying pan and heat until simmering. Add the fish, turn up the heat a little, and cook until the fish turns opaque and flaky—you might need to turn it over halfway through. Don't worry if it breaks up. Lift the fish out of the milk into a bowl and break it up roughly with a fork. Reserve the milk.

Cook the potatoes and garlic cloves in simmering water for about 12 minutes or until the potatoes are tender. Drain the potatoes and put them back in the saucepan. Peel the garlic and add to the potatoes, mash everything together, and strain in the saffron milk. Keep mashing until the mixture is smooth, then stir in the fish, flour, 1 teaspoon of lemon zest, the parsley, and the cream. Season well.

Shape the mixture into eight even-sized cakes. Put them in the refrigerator while you make the herb crème fraîche by mixing together the crème fraîche, remaining lemon zest, and herbs.

Heat the butter in a large, nonstick frying pan and cook the fish cakes for 3 minutes on each side—they should have a brown crust. Serve with the crème fraîche.

Serves 4

Stir-fried chicken with ginger and cashews

1 1/2 tablespoons vegetable oil
8 scallions, cut into pieces
3 garlic cloves, crushed
3-in. piece ginger, finely shredded
2 skinless chicken breasts, cut
    into strips
2 red bell peppers, cut into strips
1 cup snow peas
1 cup cashews
2 tablespoons soy sauce
1 1/2 teaspoons sesame oil
rice or noodles, to serve

Heat the vegetable oil in a wok until it is smoking—this will only take a few seconds. Add the scallions, garlic, and ginger and stir for a few seconds. Next, add the chicken and stir until it has turned white. Add the red peppers and keep stirring, then throw in the snow peas and cashews and stir-fry for another minute or so.

Once the red peppers have started to soften a little, add the soy sauce and sesame oil, toss everything together, and then remove the stir-fry to a serving dish.

Serve with rice or noodles and more soy sauce if you like.

Serves 4

Minestrone with pesto

1 tablespoon olive oil
1 small onion, finely chopped
1 garlic clove, finely chopped
1 tablespoon finely chopped parsley
2 oz. pancetta, cubed
1 celery stalk, halved, then sliced
1 carrot, sliced
1 teaspoon tomato paste
7-oz. can chopped tomatoes
4 cups chicken or vegetable stock
1 zucchini, sliced
2 tablespoons peas
6 green beans, cut into 3/4-in. lengths
handful of shredded savoy cabbage
2 tablespoons ditalini or other small
   pasta
1/2 cup cranberry beans, drained and
   rinsed
2 tablespoons fresh pesto

Melt the oil in a large saucepan and add the onion, garlic, parsley, and pancetta. Cook over very low heat, stirring the mixture once or twice, for about 10 minutes or until the onion is soft and golden. If your heat won't go very low, keep an eye on everything and stir more often.

Add the celery and carrot and cook them for 5 minutes. Stir in the tomato paste and chopped tomatoes with plenty of pepper. Add the stock and bring slowly to a boil. Cover and leave to simmer for 30 minutes, stirring once or twice.

Taste the soup for seasoning, adjust if necessary, then add the zucchini, peas, green beans, cabbage, ditalini, and cranberry beans. Simmer everything for a couple of minutes until the pasta is al dente. Serve with some pesto spooned into the middle of each bowl.

Serves 4

Spaghetti puttanesca

14 oz. spaghetti
2 tablespoons olive oil
1 onion, finely chopped
2 garlic cloves, finely sliced
1 small red chili, cored, seeded,
  and sliced
6 anchovy fillets, finely chopped
14-oz. can chopped tomatoes
1 tablespoon fresh oregano, finely
  chopped
16 black olives, halved and pitted
2 tablespoons small capers
handful of basil leaves

Cook the spaghetti in a large saucepan of boiling salted water until al dente, stirring once or twice to make sure the pieces are not stuck together.

Heat the olive oil in a large saucepan and add the onion, garlic, and chili. Gently fry for about 8 minutes or until the onion is soft. Add the anchovies and cook for another minute. Add the tomato, oregano, olive halves, and capers and bring to a boil. Reduce the heat, season with salt and pepper, and leave the sauce to simmer for 3 minutes.

Drain the spaghetti and add to the sauce. Toss well so that the pasta is coated in the sauce. Sprinkle with the basil, then serve.

Serves 4

Shrimp laksa

1½ tablespoons vegetable oil
4 tablespoons Malaysian laksa paste
2 cups coconut milk
2 cups chicken stock
16 shrimp, peeled and deveined
8 oz. rice vermicelli
8 tofu puffs, cut into 3 pieces
4-in. piece cucumber, shredded
4 handfuls bean sprouts
a few sprigs of Vietnamese mint
  or mint leaves
sambal oelek or hot chili paste,
  to taste
lime wedges, to serve

Heat the oil in a wok or saucepan and add the laksa paste. Depending on the brand, you may need to add a little more or less laksa paste—start with a little, make the soup base, and then stir in a bit more if you need to. Cook the paste over a medium heat, stirring it to keep it from sticking, for 2–3 minutes.

Stir in the coconut milk and chicken stock, bring the mixture to a boil, and simmer for 5 minutes. Add the shrimp, bring the mixture back to a boil, then reduce the heat and simmer for 3 minutes—the shrimp will turn pink and opaque when they are ready.

Cook the rice vermicelli in boiling water for 3 minutes. Drain and divide among four deep serving bowls.

Divide the tofu puffs, cucumber, and bean sprouts among the bowls, then ladle in the laksa mixture. Garnish the laksa with a sprig or two of mint and a small amount of sambal oelek (be careful, as it is very hot). Serve with lime wedges to squeeze into the laksa.

Serves 4

Asparagus risotto

2 lb. 4 oz. asparagus
4 cups chicken stock
4 tablespoons olive oil
1 onion, finely chopped
1²/₃ cups risotto rice
3 oz. Parmesan cheese, grated
3 tablespoons heavy cream

Wash the asparagus and remove the woody ends. Separate the tender tips from the stems.

Cook the asparagus stems in boiling water for about 8 minutes or until very tender. Drain and put in a blender with the chicken stock. Blend for 1 minute, then put in a saucepan, bring to a boil, and maintain at a low simmer.

Cook the asparagus tips in boiling water for 1 minute, drain, and rinse in ice water.

Heat the olive oil in a wide, heavy-bottomed saucepan. Add the onion and cook until softened but not browned. Add the rice and reduce the heat to low. Season and stir briefly to thoroughly coat the rice. Stir in a ladleful of the simmering stock and cook over medium heat, stirring continuously. When the stock has been absorbed, stir in another ladleful. Continue this process for about 20 minutes, until all the stock has been added and the rice is al dente.

Add the Parmesan cheese and cream and gently stir in the asparagus tips. Season with salt and pepper and serve hot.

Serves 4

Baked potatoes with arugula, fava beans, and blue cheese

4 large potatoes
coarse salt
10½ oz. fava beans
⅓ cup cream
4 oz. blue cheese, crumbled
4 handfuls arugula, chopped

Heat the oven to 400°F. Wash the potatoes and, while they are still damp, rub them with a little of the coarse salt. Prick them several times and then put them in the oven, directly on the oven rack. This will help them cook evenly. Bake for 1 hour, then squeeze them gently— they should be soft. If they are still hard, give them another 15 minutes or so.

Cook the fava beans in boiling water for 3 minutes, then drain them well. Peel off the outer gray skins.

When the potatoes are cooked, cut a cross in one side of each and squeeze the potatoes around the middle until they open up.

Put the cream in a small saucepan, add the fava beans, cook them gently for a minute or two, then add the blue cheese and arugula. Stir everything together, and when the arugula has wilted, spoon the mixture into the potatoes. Season with black pepper.

Serves 4

Salmon kedgeree

4 cups fish stock
14-oz. salmon fillet
3 tablespoons butter
2 tablespoons vegetable oil
1 onion, chopped
2 teaspoons madras curry paste
1 cup long-grain rice
2 hard-boiled eggs, cut into wedges
3 tablespoons chopped parsley
   leaves
3 tablespoons cream
lemon wedges, to serve

Put the stock in a frying pan and bring to a boil. Put the salmon in the stock, cover, then reduce the heat to a simmer. Cook for 3 minutes or until it becomes firm when pressed and turns opaque. Lift out the salmon and flake it into large pieces by gently pulling it apart.

Melt half of the butter in a frying pan with the oil, add the onion, and cook over low heat until the onion softens and turns translucent. Stir in the curry paste, then add the rice and mix well until the rice is coated. Add the fish stock, mix well, then bring the mixture to a boil.

Simmer the rice, covered, over very low heat for 8 minutes, then add the salmon and cook, covered, for another 5 minutes, until all the liquid is absorbed. If the rice is too dry and not completely cooked, add a splash of boiling water and keep cooking for another 1–2 minutes.

Stir in the rest of the butter, the eggs, parsley, and cream (you can leave out the cream if you prefer—the result won't be as rich). Serve with lemon wedges to squeeze over the kedgeree.

Serves 4

Spicy sausages with harissa and couscous

2 tablespoons butter
1½ cups instant couscous
2 teaspoons harissa
¼ cup olive oil
2 tablespoons lemon juice
1½ tablespoons grated lemon zest
2 tablespoons parsley, chopped
1 cup roasted red bell pepper, sliced
⅓ cup raisins
12 merguez sausages
plain yogurt, to serve

Put the butter in a saucepan with 2 cups water and bring to a boil. Stir in the couscous, then remove from the heat. Put a lid on the pan and leave it to sit for 5 minutes. Turn on the broiler. Stir the harissa, olive oil, lemon juice, and zest together until well mixed. Add the parsley, red pepper, and raisins and leave everything to marinate briefly.

Grill the sausages for 8 minutes, turning them so they brown on all sides.

Meanwhile, take the lid off the couscous, stir it for a minute or two to separate the grains, then stir in the harissa mixture.

Serve the couscous with the sausages sliced over it, topped with a large dollop of yogurt.

Serves 4

Roast tomato risotto

4 cups chicken or vegetable stock
pinch of saffron threads
1 cup dry white wine
2 tablespoons butter
1 onion, finely chopped
1 1/3 cups risotto rice
1 tablespoon olive oil
1 garlic clove, crushed
40 cherry tomatoes
Parmesan cheese, grated
4 tablespoons parsley, finely chopped

Heat the stock in a saucepan until it is simmering, then leave it over low heat. Put the saffron into the wine and let soak.

Melt the butter in a large, deep, heavy-bottomed frying pan, then gently cook the onion until it is soft, but not browned. Add the rice, turn the heat to low, and stir well to coat all the grains of rice with the butter.

Add the wine and saffron to the rice, turn the heat up to medium, and cook, stirring, until all the liquid has been absorbed. Add the hot stock, a few ladles at a time, stirring continuously so that the rice cooks evenly and releases some of its starch.

While the rice is cooking, heat the oil in a saucepan, add the garlic and tomatoes, then fry for 2–3 minutes over medium heat, until the tomatoes are slightly soft and have burst open. Season well.

Once all the stock has been added to the rice, taste the rice to see if it is al dente. Stir in 4 tablespoons of Parmesan and the parsley. Spoon the tomatoes over the top and sprinkle with some more Parmesan. Serve immediately.

Serves 4

Hamburgers with fresh corn relish

1 lb. 9 oz. ground beef
1 garlic clove
1½ onions, very finely chopped
2 tablespoons Italian parsley, finely
  chopped
1 tablespoon tomato ketchup
¼ teaspoon Worcestershire sauce
2 ears corn
2 tomatoes, finely chopped
1 tablespoon sweet chili sauce
handful of cilantro leaves
lime juice
1 tablespoon vegetable oil
4 hamburger buns
romaine lettuce leaves, to serve

Preheat the broiler. Put the beef in a bowl with the garlic, half of the onion, the parsley, tomato ketchup, and the Worcestershire sauce. Season and mix well, then leave it to marinate while you make the relish.

Broil the ears of corn on all sides until slightly blackened and charred around the edges. By this time it should be cooked through. Slice off the kernels by slicing down the length of the cobs with a sharp knife. Mix the kernels with the tomato, chili sauce, cilantro, and remaining onion. Add lime juice and salt and pepper to taste.

Form the beef mixture into four large patties and flatten them out to the size of the buns (bear in mind that they will shrink as they cook).

Heat the oil in a frying pan and fry the beef patties for 3–5 minutes on each side, depending on how well cooked you like them. While they are cooking, toast the buns.

Place a lettuce leaf or two on each bun base, add some relish, and top with a hamburger patty and the bun top. Serve any extra relish on the side.

Serves 4

Roast new potatoes with sweet chili dip

1 lb. 5 oz. new potatoes
1 1/2 tablespoons olive oil
2 teaspoons thyme leaves
2 teaspoons coarse salt
1/3 cup sweet chili sauce
1/3 cup sour cream
2 scallions, finely chopped

Preheat the oven to 400°F. If any of your potatoes are too big to eat in more than two bites, cut them in half. Put them in a roasting pan with the oil, thyme, and salt and mix so they are coated. Roast for 30–40 minutes or until the potatoes are cooked through.

Mix the sweet chili sauce, sour cream, and scallions together. Serve with the potatoes for dipping.

Serves 4

Tandoori chicken with cardamom rice

1 cup plain yogurt, plus extra for
  serving
¼ cup tandoori paste
2 tablespoons lemon juice
2 lb. 4 oz. chicken breast fillets, cut
  into 1½-in. cubes
1 tablespoon vegetable oil
1 onion, finely diced
1½ cups long-grain rice
2 cardamom pods, bruised
3 cups hot chicken stock
14 oz. spinach leaves

Soak eight wooden skewers in water for 30 minutes to prevent them from burning during cooking. Combine the yogurt, tandoori paste, and lemon juice in a nonmetallic dish. Add the chicken and coat well, then cover and marinate for at least 10 minutes.

Heat the oil in a saucepan. Add the onion and cook for 3 minutes, then add the rice and cardamom pods. Cook, stirring often, for 3–5 minutes or until the rice is slightly opaque. Add the hot chicken stock and bring to a boil. Reduce the heat to low, cover, and cook the rice, without removing the lid, for 15 minutes.

Heat a broiler or grill to very hot. Thread the chicken cubes onto the skewers, leaving the bottom quarter of the skewers empty. Cook on each side for 5 minutes or until cooked through.

Wash the spinach and put in a large saucepan with just the water clinging to the leaves. Cook, covered, over medium heat for 1–2 minutes or until the spinach has wilted. Uncover the rice, fluff up with a fork, and serve with the spinach, chicken, and extra yogurt.

Serves 4

Grilled eggplant with ricotta and tomatoes

2 eggplants, sliced
1/3 cup olive oil
1 lb. 2 oz. cherry tomatoes, halved
2 garlic cloves, crushed
2 teaspoons capers, drained
1/2 cup ricotta cheese
small basil leaves, to garnish

Preheat the broiler. Brush the eggplant slices with some of the oil. Grill the slices on both sides until they are brown, then lay them in a large, shallow baking dish that will fit under the broiler.

Heat the rest of the oil in a small saucepan, add the cherry tomatoes and garlic, then fry briefly until the tomatoes just start to soften. Add the capers for a minute. Pour the tomatoes over the eggplant, season well, and spoon the ricotta on top. Put the dish back under the broiler until the ricotta starts to bubble, then sprinkle the basil leaves over the top.

Serves 4

Ham braised with Belgian endive

1 1/2 tablespoons vegetable oil
2 teaspoons butter
4 heads Belgian endive, sliced
  horizontally
8 thick slices ham
2 teaspoons brown sugar
3/4 cup white wine
2 tablespoons chopped parsley

Heat the oil in a large frying pan, add the butter, and, when it is sizzling, add the endive with the cut side down and fry for a minute. Add the slices of ham and fry them briefly on each side, moving the endive to one side. Add the sugar and wine to the pan, season well, and cover it with a lid. Cook for about 3 minutes or until the endive is soft.

Remove the lid from the pan, turn the heat up, and let the sauce bubble until it has thickened and become sticky. Stir in the parsley.

Serves 4

Cauliflower rarebits

8 thick slices ciabatta
1 garlic clove
1 lb. 12 oz. cauliflower, cut into small
  florets
1 cup grated Gruyère cheese
1 cup grated cheddar cheese
1 tablespoon Dijon mustard
2 eggs, beaten
2 tablespoons beer
4 tablespoons cream

Turn on the broiler and toast the
ciabatta. Cut the garlic clove in half
and rub the cut sides over one side
of each slice of ciabatta.

Bring a saucepan of water to a boil
and cook the cauliflower for about
5 minutes or until it is tender when
you prod it with a knife. Drain well.

Mix the cheeses, mustard, egg, beer,
and cream together. Put the toast
on a baking tray and arrange some
cauliflower on top of each piece.
Divide the cheese mixture among the
pieces of toast, making sure all all the
cauliflower is coated.

Put the rarebits under the broiler until
they are brown and bubbling.

Serves 4

Chicken casserole with olives and tomatoes

1 tablespoon olive oil
1 large onion, chopped
2 garlic cloves, crushed
8 pieces chicken, skin left on
1 tablespoon tomato paste
1½ cups white wine
pinch of sugar
8 large ripe tomatoes, chopped
4 tablespoons parsley, chopped
1 cup green beans, trimmed and
   halved
¾ cup olives

Heat the oil in a large, flameproof casserole and fry the onion for a minute or two. Add the garlic and the chicken and fry for as long as it takes to brown the chicken all over.

Add the tomato paste and white wine, along with the sugar, and stir everything together. Add the tomato and any juices, the parsley, and the beans and bring to a boil. Turn down the heat, season well, and simmer for 40 minutes.

Add the olives and simmer for another 5 minutes. The sauce should be thick by now and the chicken fully cooked. Add more salt and pepper if needed. Serve with potatoes, pasta, or rice.

Serves 4

Salsicce with white beans and gremolata

3 tablespoons olive oil
12 salsicce or thick pork sausages,
  cut into chunks
6 garlic cloves, smashed
1²/₃ cups grilled red or yellow bell
  pepper strips
2 (14-oz.) cans cannellini beans,
  drained and rinsed
1½ tablespoons grated lemon zest
6 tablespoons parsley, chopped
2 tablespoons lemon juice
extra-virgin olive oil, for drizzling

Heat the olive oil in a frying pan and cook the salsicce until they are browned all over and cooked through. Lift them out of the frying pan with a slotted spoon and set aside.

Put three garlic cloves in the frying pan and cook them over low heat until they are very soft. Add the pepper strips to the pan along with the beans and salsicce. Stir together and cook over low heat for 2 minutes to heat through. Season well with salt and pepper.

To make the gremolata, smash the remaining three garlic cloves to a paste, with a little salt, in a mortar and pestle. Mix in the lemon zest and the chopped parsley and season with salt and pepper.

Just before serving, stir the gremolata into the beans and then finish the dish with the lemon juice and a drizzle of olive oil.

Serves 4

Stir-fried tofu with oyster sauce

1 lb. 2 oz. firm tofu
3–4 tablespoons vegetable oil
2 garlic cloves, crushed
2 teaspoons grated ginger
2 tablespoons oyster sauce
2 tablespoons soy sauce
2 teaspoons sugar
8 oyster mushrooms, quartered
2 scallions, cut into pieces
2 baby bok choy, quartered
large handful of cilantro leaves

Cut the tofu into bite-sized pieces. Heat a wok over a medium heat, add half the oil, and heat until it is very hot and almost smoking. Cook half the tofu until golden brown on all sides, making sure you move it gently or it will stick and break. Remove from the pan and repeat with the remaining oil and tofu. Return the tofu to the pan.

Add the garlic, ginger, oyster sauce, soy sauce, and sugar, then toss until well combined. Add the oyster mushrooms, scallions, and bok choy, then simmer until the sauce has reduced a little and the scallions and bok choy have softened slightly. Garnish with the cilantro leaves.

Serves 4

Chive gnocchi with blue cheese

2 lb. (about 6 medium) floury potatoes
  (e.g., russet)
2²/₃ cups all-purpose flour
2 tablespoons chives, chopped
4 egg yolks
3¹/₄ oz. blue cheese
²/₃ cup cream

Peel the potatoes and cut them into even pieces. Cook them in simmering water for 20 minutes or until they are tender. Drain them very well, then mash them in a large bowl. Add 2 cups of the flour, the chives, and egg yolks, along with some salt and pepper, and mix well. Add enough of the remaining flour to make a mixture that is soft but not sticky. Divide the mixture into four, roll each bit into a sausage shape ¹/₂ in. across and cut off lengths about ¹/₂ in. long. You don't need to shape the gnocchi any more than this.

Bring a large saucepan of water to a boil and cook the gnocchi in batches. As they rise to the surface (they will do this when cooked through), scoop them out with a slotted spoon and drain well.

While the gnocchi are cooking, put the blue cheese and cream in a saucepan and gently heat. Put the gnocchi in a large bowl and pour the blue cheese sauce over it. Gently fold the sauce into the gnocchi and serve.

Serves 4

Pastitsio

2 tablespoons vegetable oil
4 garlic cloves, crushed
2 onions, chopped
2 lb. 4 oz. ground beef
2 lb. 4 oz. canned peeled tomatoes, chopped
1 cup dry red wine
1 cup beef stock
1 bay leaf
1 teaspoon dried mixed herbs
12 oz. ziti pasta
3 eggs, lightly beaten
2 1/4 cups plain yogurt
7 oz. kefalotyri cheese, grated
1/2 teaspoon ground nutmeg
1/2 cup grated cheddar cheese
oakleaf lettuce, to serve

Heat the oil in a large heavy-bottomed pan and cook the garlic and onion over medium heat for 5 minutes or until the onion is soft. Add the beef and cook over high heat until browned, then drain off any excess fat. Add the tomato, wine, stock, bay leaf and herbs and bring to a boil. Reduce the heat and simmer for 40 minutes. Season well.

Preheat the oven to 350°F. Cook the pasta in a large pan of rapidly boiling water until al dente. Drain well and spread in the bottom of a large ovenproof dish. Pour in half the egg and top with the sauce.

Combine the yogurt, remaining egg, kefalotyri, and nutmeg and pour over the top. Sprinkle with the cheddar and bake for 40 minutes or until golden brown. Leave to stand for 10 minutes before serving with oakleaf lettuce.

Serves 6–8

Spinach and ricotta ravioli

1 tablespoon olive oil
1 red onion, finely chopped
1 garlic clove, crushed
about 6 handfuls spinach leaves,
  coarsely chopped
1 cup ricotta cheese
2 egg yolks, beaten
2 tablespoons grated Parmesan
  cheese
freshly grated nutmeg
48 wonton wrappers
2 tablespoons butter
2 tablespoons sage leaves

Heat the oil in a frying pan, add the onion and garlic, and fry them over low heat for a few minutes until the onion is soft and translucent. Add the spinach and stir until it wilts.

Stir the spinach mixture into the ricotta, along with the egg yolk, Parmesan, nutmeg to taste, and some salt and pepper.

Brush a little water around the edge of a wonton wrapper and put a teaspoon of filling in the center. Fold the wrapper over to make a half-moon shape and press the edges firmly together. Put the ravioli on a towel laid out on your work surface and repeat with the remaining wrappers.

Bring a large saucepan of water to a boil and cook the ravioli for a few minutes. They will float to the surface when they are ready. Scoop them out carefully with a slotted spoon and drain them in a colander. Melt the butter in a small saucepan, add the sage, and sizzle for a few minutes until the butter browns slightly. Put the ravioli in bowls and pour the butter and sage over them.

Serves 4

Egg-fried rice

4 eggs
1 scallion, chopped
1/3 cup fresh or frozen peas (optional)
3 tablespoons vegetable oil
4 cups cooked long-grain rice

Beat the eggs with a pinch of salt and 1 teaspoon of the scallion. Cook the peas in a pan of simmering water for 3 minutes if fresh or 1 minute if frozen.

Heat a wok over high heat, add the oil, and heat until very hot. Reduce the heat, add the eggs, and lightly scramble. Add the rice before the eggs are completely set. Increase the heat, then stir to separate the rice grains and break the eggs into small pieces. Add the peas and the remaining scallion, then season with salt. Stir constantly for 1 minute.

Serves 4

Grilled nachos

2 (10½-oz.) bags corn tortilla chips
4 tomatoes, chopped
1 red onion, finely chopped
3 jalapeño chilies, thinly sliced
2 tablespoons lime juice
4 tablespoons chopped cilantro
  leaves
1½ cups feta cheese, crumbled

Preheat the broiler. Arrange the tortilla chips on four ovenproof plates.

Sprinkle the tomatoes, onion, and jalapeño chilies on top of the tortilla chips, then drizzle with the lime juice and season with some salt. Sprinkle the cilantro and feta cheese over the chips, making sure they are well covered.

Grill the nachos until they start to brown around the edges and the cheese starts to melt. Serve hot but be careful of the plates—they will be very hot too.

Serves 4

Ramen noodle soup with char siu

8 nests of dried thin ramen egg
  noodles
4 cups chicken stock
4 scallions, shredded
4 tablespoons soy sauce
1 lb. char siu (Chinese roast pork)
2 small bok choy, roughly chopped
sesame oil, for drizzling

Cook the noodles in a large saucepan of boiling water for about 4 minutes or until they are just cooked, stirring once or twice to make sure they are not stuck together. The cooking time will vary depending on the brand of noodles.

Bring the chicken stock to a boil in a saucepan, then add the scallions and soy sauce. Taste the stock to see if it has enough flavor and, if not, add a bit more soy sauce—don't overdo it, though, as the soup's base should be quite mild. Turn the heat down to a simmer. Cut the char siu into bite-size shreds or slices (small enough to pick up and eat with chopsticks).

Drain the noodles and divide them among four bowls. Add the bok choy to the chicken stock, stir in, then divide the stock and vegetables among the four bowls. Arrange the char siu on top, then drizzle a little sesame oil onto each—sesame oil has a very strong flavor, so you will only need a few drops for each bowl.

Serves 4

Hot and sweet chicken

½ cup rice vinegar
⅔ cup superfine sugar
6 garlic cloves, crushed
large pinch of red pepper flakes
1 teaspoon ground coriander
1 teaspoon ground white pepper
2 bunches cilantro, finely chopped,
   including roots and stems
3 tablespoons olive oil
2 tablespoons lemon juice
8 boneless and skinless chicken
   thighs, cut in half
2 tablespoons superfine sugar, extra
2 tablespoons fish sauce
1 small cucumber, peeled and sliced

Put the vinegar and sugar in a small saucepan, bring to a boil, then turn down the heat and simmer for a minute. Take the mixture off the heat and add two crushed garlic cloves, the red pepper flakes, and a pinch of salt. Let cool.

Heat a small frying pan, add the ground coriander and white pepper, and stir for a minute. This will make the spices more fragrant. Add the rest of the garlic, the fresh cilantro, and a pinch of salt. Add 2 tablespoons of the oil and all the lemon juice and mix to a paste. Rub this all over the chicken pieces.

Heat the rest of the oil in a wok, add the chicken, and fry it on both sides for 8 minutes or until it is cooked through. Sprinkle in the extra sugar and the fish sauce and cook for another minute or two until any excess liquid has evaporated and the chicken pieces are sticky. Serve the chicken with the sliced cucumber and some rice. Dress with the sauce.

Serves 4

Lamb pilaf

1 large eggplant, cut into $\frac{1}{2}$-in. cubes
$\frac{1}{2}$ cup olive oil
1 large onion, finely chopped
1 teaspoon ground cinnamon
2 teaspoons ground cumin
1 teaspoon ground coriander
1 $\frac{1}{2}$ cups long-grain rice
2 cups chicken or vegetable stock
1 lb. 2 oz. ground lamb
$\frac{1}{2}$ teaspoon allspice
2 tablespoons olive oil, extra
2 tomatoes, cut into wedges
3 tablespoons toasted pistachios
2 tablespoons currants
2 tablespoons chopped cilantro
   leaves, to garnish

Put the eggplant in a colander, sprinkle with salt, and let stand for 1 hour to drain. Rinse and squeeze dry. Heat 2 tablespoons of the oil in a large, deep frying pan with a lid, add the eggplant, and cook over medium heat for 8–10 minutes. Drain on paper towels.

Heat the remaining oil, add the onion, and cook for 4–5 minutes or until soft. Stir in half each of the cinnamon, cumin, and ground coriander. Add the rice and stir to coat, then add the stock, season, and bring to a boil. Reduce the heat and simmer, covered, for 15 minutes.

Put the ground lamb in a bowl with the allspice and remaining cumin, cinnamon, and ground coriander. Season with salt and pepper and mix. Roll into balls the size of marbles. Heat the extra oil in the frying pan and cook the meatballs in batches over medium heat for 5 minutes each batch. Drain on paper towels.

Add the tomatoes to the pan and cook for 3–5 minutes or until golden. Remove from the pan. Stir the eggplant, pistachios, currants, and meatballs through the rice. Serve the pilaf with the tomatoes and cilantro.

Serves 4

203

Saffron chicken and rice

¼ cup olive oil
4 chicken thighs and 6 drumsticks
1 large red onion, finely chopped
1 large green bell pepper, two-thirds
  diced and one-third julienned
3 teaspoons sweet paprika
14-oz. can chopped tomatoes
1¼ cups long-grain rice
½ teaspoon ground saffron

Heat 2 tablespoons of the oil in a deep frying pan over high heat. Season the chicken pieces well and brown in batches. Remove the chicken from the pan.

Reduce the heat to medium and add the remaining oil. Add the onion and diced pepper and cook gently for 5 minutes. Stir in the paprika and cook for about 30 seconds. Add the tomatoes and simmer for 1–3 minutes or until the mixture thickens.

Stir 3½ cups of boiling water into the pan, then add the rice and saffron. Return the chicken to the pan and stir to combine. Season with salt and pepper. Bring to a boil, cover, reduce the heat to medium–low, and simmer for 20 minutes or until all the liquid has been absorbed and the chicken is tender. Stir in the julienned pepper, then let it stand, covered, for 3–4 minutes before serving.

Serves 4

Porcini and walnut pasta

½ oz. dried porcini
14 oz. penne pasta
2 tablespoons olive oil
1 onion, finely chopped
2 garlic cloves, crushed
24 button mushrooms, sliced
3 thyme sprigs
1 cup walnuts
2 tablespoons sour cream
Parmesan cheese, grated

Put the porcini in a bowl with just enough boiling water to cover them, and let soak for half an hour. If they soak up all the water quickly, add a little more.

Cook the penne in a large saucepan of boiling salted water until it is al dente, stirring once or twice to make sure the pieces are not stuck together.

Heat the oil in a deep frying pan and fry the onion and garlic together until translucent but not browned. Add the porcini and any soaking liquid, mushrooms, and thyme, and continue frying. The mushrooms will give off liquid as they cook, so continue cooking until the liquid is reabsorbed.

In a separate pan, dry-fry the walnuts without any oil until they start to brown and smell toasted. When they have cooled down a bit, roughly chop, then add them to the frying pan. Toss with the drained penne, stir the sour cream through, and season well. Serve with the Parmesan.

Serves 4

Classic jambalaya

2 tablespoons olive oil
1 large red onion, finely chopped
1 garlic clove, crushed
2 slices bacon, finely chopped
1 1/2 cups long-grain rice
1 red bell pepper, diced
5 1/2 oz. ham, chopped
14-oz. can chopped tomatoes
14-oz. jar tomato pasta sauce
1 teaspoon Worcestershire sauce
dash of hot pepper sauce
1/2 teaspoon dried thyme
1/2 cup chopped parsley
5 1/2 oz. cooked, peeled, small shrimp
4 scallions, thinly sliced

Heat the oil in a large saucepan over medium heat. Add the onion, garlic, and bacon and cook, stirring, for 5 minutes or until the onion is softened but not browned. Stir in the rice and cook for another 5 minutes or until lightly golden.

Add the pepper, ham, tomatoes, tomato sauce, Worcestershire, hot pepper sauce, and thyme and stir until well combined. Bring the mixture to a boil, then reduce the heat to low. Cook, covered, for 30–40 minutes or until the rice is tender.

Stir in the parsley and shrimp and season with salt and freshly ground black pepper. Sprinkle with the scallions, then serve.

Serves 4–6

Thai basil fried rice

2 tablespoons vegetable oil
3 shallots, sliced
1 garlic clove, finely chopped
1 small red chili, finely chopped
3/4 cup green beans, cut into short
  pieces
1 small red bell pepper, julienned
1 cup button mushrooms, halved
2 1/2 cups cooked jasmine rice
1 teaspoon brown sugar
3 tablespoons light soy sauce
1/4 cup fresh Thai basil, shredded
1 tablespoon cilantro leaves, chopped
fried shallot flakes, to garnish
Thai basil leaves, to garnish

Heat a wok over high heat, add the oil, and swirl. Stir-fry the shallots, garlic, and chili for 3 minutes or until the shallots start to brown. Add the beans, red pepper, and mushrooms, stir-fry for 3 minutes or until cooked, then stir in the cooked jasmine rice and heat through.

Dissolve the brown sugar in the soy sauce, then pour over the rice. Stir in the herbs. Garnish with the shallot flakes and basil.

Serves 4

Roast vegetables with poached egg and Camembert

12 pearl onions or shallots
1/3 cup olive oil
2 bundles asparagus, cut into
   1 1/2-in. pieces
4 zucchini, thickly sliced
2 eggplants, cubed
8 garlic cloves
2 tablespoons lemon juice
4 eggs
9 oz. Camembert cheese, cubed

Preheat the oven on to 400°F. Peel the onions, leaving them attached at the root end. Don't leave any root on.

Put the oil in a roasting pan and add the onions, asparagus, zucchini, and eggplant, along with the garlic, and toss well. Season with salt and black pepper. Put the pan in the oven and roast the vegetables for 20 minutes. Sprinkle with the lemon juice and roast for another 10 minutes.

Put a large frying pan full of water over high heat and bring it to a boil. When the water is bubbling, turn the heat down to a gentle simmer. Crack an egg into a cup and slip the egg into the water—it should start to turn opaque. Do the same with the other eggs, keeping them separate. Turn the heat down as low as you can and leave the eggs to cook for 3 minutes.

Divide the vegetables between four ovenproof dishes. Put the Camembert on top of the vegetables, dividing it among the dishes. Put the dishes back in the oven for a couple of minutes to melt the cheese.

Top each dish with a poached egg and some black pepper.

Serves 4

Chili linguine with chermoula chicken

1 lb. 5 oz. chicken breast fillets
1 lb. 2 oz. chili-flavored linguine

Chermoula
2 cups cilantro leaves, chopped
2 cups Italian parsley, chopped
4 garlic cloves, crushed
2 teaspoons ground cumin
2 teaspoons ground paprika
1/2 cup lemon juice
2 teaspoons lemon zest
1/2 cup olive oil

Heat a large nonstick frying pan over medium heat. Add the chicken breasts and cook until tender. Remove from the pan and leave for 5 minutes before cutting into thin slices.

Cook the pasta in a large saucepan of rapidly boiling salted water until al dente, then drain.

Meanwhile, combine the chermoula ingredients in a glass bowl and add the sliced chicken. Let stand until the pasta has finished cooking. Serve the pasta topped with the chermoula chicken.

Serves 4

Green chicken curry

1 cup coconut cream
4 tablespoons green curry paste
8 skinless chicken thighs or 4 chicken
  breasts, cut into pieces
1 cup coconut milk
4 Thai eggplants or ½ of a purple
  eggplant, cut into chunks
2 tablespoons brown sugar
2 tablespoons fish sauce
4 kaffir lime leaves, torn
handful of Thai basil leaves
1–2 large red chilies, sliced
coconut milk or cream, for drizzling
rice, to serve

Place a wok over low heat, add the coconut cream, and let it come to a boil. Stir it for a while until the oil separates out. Don't let it burn.

Add the green curry paste, stir for a minute, then add the chicken. Cook the chicken until it turns opaque, then add the coconut milk and eggplant. Cook for a minute or two until the eggplant is tender. Add the sugar, fish sauce, lime leaves, and half of the basil, then mix together.

Garnish with the rest of the basil, the chili, and a drizzle of coconut milk or cream. Serve with rice.

Serves 4

Meatball and white bean soup

1 lb. 5 oz. ground beef
2 garlic cloves, crushed
1 tablespoon parsley, finely chopped
large pinch of ground cinnamon
large pinch of freshly grated nutmeg
2 eggs, lightly beaten
6 cups beef stock
2 carrots, thinly sliced
2 (14-oz.) cans white beans, drained
1/2 head of savoy cabbage, finely
  shredded
Parmesan cheese, grated

Put the beef in a bowl with the garlic, parsley, cinnamon, nutmeg, and half of the egg. Mix together well and season with salt and pepper. If the mixture is dry, add the rest of the egg — you want it to be sticky enough so that forming small balls is easy.

Roll the beef mixture into bite-size balls. Put them on a plate as you make them.

Put the beef stock in a saucepan with the carrot and bring it to a boil. Add the meatballs, one at a time, and turn the heat down to a simmer. Test one of the balls after 3 minutes. It should be cooked through; if it isn't, cook a little longer. Add the beans and cabbage and cook for another 4–5 minutes. Season the broth to taste with salt and pepper.

Serve the soup with lots of Parmesan stirred in and plenty of bread to dunk into the broth.

Serves 4

Sweet-and-sour pork

1 lb. 4 oz. pork loin, cubed
2 eggs
6 tablespoons cornstarch
1 tablespoon vegetable oil
1 onion, cubed
1 red bell pepper, cubed
2 scallions, cut into lengths
1 cup clear rice vinegar or white
   wine vinegar
1/3 cup tomato ketchup
1 cup sugar
2 tablespoons vegetable oil, extra

Put the pork cubes and egg in a bowl with 4 tablespoons of the cornstarch. Stir everything around to coat the pork well, then place in a sieve and shake off any excess cornstarch.

Heat a wok over high heat, add a tablespoon of oil, and heat it until it just starts to smoke. Add the onion and cook it for a minute. Add the red pepper and scallions and cook for another minute. Add the vinegar, tomato ketchup, and sugar, turn down the heat, and stir together until the sugar dissolves. Bring to a boil and simmer it for about 3 minutes.

Mix 2 tablespoons of cornstarch with 2 tablespoons of water, add it to the sweet-and-sour mixture, then simmer for a minute until the sauce thickens a bit. Pour the sauce into a bowl.

Heat half the remaining oil in a nonstick frying pan over a medium heat. As soon as the oil is hot, add half the pork cubes into the pan and cook them until they are browned and crisp. Remove the cooked pork from the pan. Repeat with the remaining oil and pork. Return all the cooked pork to the pan and add the sauce. Reheat until the sauce is bubbling.

Serves 4

Nasi goreng

2 eggs
1/3 cup vegetable oil
3 garlic cloves, finely chopped
1 onion, finely chopped
2 red chilies, seeded and very finely
　chopped
1 teaspoon shrimp paste
1 teaspoon coriander seeds
1/2 teaspoon sugar
14 oz. raw shrimp, peeled and
　deveined
7 oz. rump steak, finely sliced
1 cup long-grain rice, cooked and
　cooled
2 teaspoons kecap manis
1 tablespoon soy sauce
4 scallions, finely chopped
1/2 head lettuce, finely shredded
1 cucumber, thinly sliced
3 tablespoons crisp fried onions

Beat the eggs and 1/4 teaspoon of salt until foamy. Heat a frying pan and brush with a little oil. Pour about one-quarter of the mixture into the pan and cook for 1–2 minutes over medium heat or until the omelette sets. Turn the omelette over and cook the other side for about 30 seconds. Remove the omelette from the pan and repeat with the remaining mixture. When the omelettes are cold, roll them up, cut into fine strips, and set aside.

Combine the garlic, onion, chili, shrimp paste, coriander, and sugar in a food processor and process until a paste is formed.

Heat 1–2 tablespoons of the oil in a wok; add the paste and cook over high heat for 1 minute. Add the shrimp and steak and stir-fry for 2–3 minutes.

Add the remaining oil and the cold rice to the wok. Stir-fry until the rice is heated through. Add the kecap manis, soy sauce, and scallions and stir-fry for another minute.

Arrange the lettuce around the outside of a large platter. Put the rice in the center and garnish with the omelette, cucumber slices, and crisp fried onion. Serve immediately.

Serves 4

Linguine with roasted cherry tomatoes

14 oz. linguine
1 lb. 2 oz. red cherry tomatoes
1 lb. 2 oz. yellow cherry tomatoes
2 tablespoons olive oil
2 garlic cloves, crushed
4 scallions, sliced
1 bunch chives, finely chopped
20 black olives
extra-virgin olive oil, for drizzling

Cook the linguine in a large saucepan of boiling salted water until al dente, stirring once or twice to make sure the pieces are not stuck together.

Cut all the cherry tomatoes in half. Heat the oil in a saucepan, add the garlic and scallions, and let them sizzle briefly. Add the cherry tomatoes and cook them over high heat until they just start to collapse and give off their juices. Add the chives and olives, season with salt and pepper, and toss together well.

Drain the linguine and put it in a large serving bowl or individual bowls. Pour the cherry tomato mixture on top and grind some black pepper over them. Drizzle with a little bit more olive oil if you like.

Serves 4

Chili

1 cup black beans or kidney beans
3 tablespoons vegetable oil
1 red onion, finely chopped
2 garlic cloves, crushed
1½ bunches cilantro, finely chopped
2 chilies, seeded and finely chopped
2 lb. 10 oz. chuck steak, cut into
   cubes
1 lb. 5 oz. canned chopped tomatoes
1½ tablespoons tomato paste
1½ cups beef stock
1½ red bell peppers, cut into squares
1 large ripe tomato, chopped
1 avocado, diced
2 limes, juiced
4 tablespoons sour cream

Put the beans in a saucepan, cover with water, bring to a boil, then turn down the heat and simmer for 10 minutes. Turn off the heat and let stand for 2 hours, then drain and rinse.

Heat half of the oil in a large, heatproof casserole dish. Cook three-quarters of the onion, all of the garlic, half of the cilantro, and the chilies for 5 minutes.

Remove the onion from the casserole dish and set aside. Heat half the remaining oil in the dish, add half the steak, and cook until well browned. Repeat with the remaining oil and steak. Return the onions and meat to the pan. Add the beans, canned tomatoes, and tomato paste and stir together. Bring to a boil, then reduce to a simmer. Put the lid on and cook it for 1 hour and 20 minutes. Add the red pepper to the casserole, stir it in, and cook for another 40 minutes.

To make the topping, mix half the remaining cilantro, the chopped tomato, avocado, and onion. Season with salt and pepper and add half of the lime juice.

When the meat is tender, add the rest of the cilantro and lime juice and season well. Serve with the topping and a dollop of sour cream.

Serves 4

Lamb curry

2 lb. 4 oz. lamb leg or shoulder,
  cubed
1/3 cup plain yogurt
2 onions, chopped
2 green chilies, roughly chopped
2 garlic cloves, crushed
3/4-in. piece ginger, grated
1/3 cup cashews
4 tablespoons korma curry paste
2 tablespoons vegetable oil
rice, to serve

Put the lamb in a bowl with half the yogurt and mix together until all the meat cubes are coated.

Put the onion, chili, garlic, ginger, cashews, and curry paste in a blender, add 1/3 cup water, and process to a smooth paste. If you don't have a blender, finely chop everything before adding the water.

Heat the oil in a flameproof casserole dish over medium heat. Add the blended mixture, season with salt, and cook over low heat for 1 minute or until the liquid evaporates and the sauce thickens. Add the lamb and slowly bring everything to a boil. Cover the casserole tightly, simmer for 1 hour and 15 minutes, then add the rest of the yogurt and keep cooking for another 30 minutes or until the meat is very tender. Stir the meat occasionally to prevent it from sticking to the pan. The sauce should be quite thick. Serve with rice.

Serves 4

Grilled chicken with pepper couscous

1 cup instant couscous
1 tablespoon olive oil
1 onion, finely chopped
2 zucchini, sliced
½ red or yellow bell pepper, roasted
  and chopped
12 sun-dried tomatoes, chopped
½ tablespoon grated orange zest
1 cup orange juice
large handful of chopped mint
8 chicken thighs or 4 chicken breasts,
  skin left on
2 tablespoons butter, softened

Preheat the broiler. Meanwhile, bring 2 cups water to a boil in a saucepan, stir in the couscous, then take the pan off the heat and let stand for 10 minutes.

Heat the oil in a frying pan and fry the onion and zucchini until lightly browned. Add the pepper and sun-dried tomatoes, then stir in the couscous. Stir in the orange zest, one-third of the orange juice, and the mint.

Put the chicken in a large, shallow baking dish in a single layer and dot it with the butter. Sprinkle with the remaining orange juice and season well with salt and pepper. Broil the chicken for 8 to 10 minutes, turning it over halfway through. The skin should be browned and crisp.

Serve the chicken on the couscous, with any juices poured over it.

Serves 4

Shepherd's pie

1 tablespoon vegetable oil
1 onion, finely chopped
1 carrot, finely chopped
2 lb. 4 oz. ground lamb, raw or
  cooked
all-purpose flour, for thickening
2 tablespoons tomato ketchup
2 beef bouillon cubes
Worcestershire sauce
6 potatoes, cut into chunks
1/3 cup milk
butter, for topping
peas, to serve

Preheat the oven to 400°F. Heat the oil in a frying pan, add the onion and carrot, and fry until they begin to brown around the edges. Add the meat and cook, turning over every now and then, breaking up any large lumps with the back of a fork.

When the meat is browned all over, add a little flour, about a teaspoon, and stir it in. Add the ketchup and the beef bouillon cubes. Add about 2 cups of water and mix everything together. Bring the mixture to a boil, then turn down the heat and simmer gently for about 30 minutes or until thick. Season with salt, pepper, and Worcestershire sauce.

While the meat is cooking, cook the potatoes in simmering water until they are tender (about 12 minutes). When they are soft, drain and mash them with the milk and plenty of seasoning. Place the meat in a large ovenproof dish or four individual dishes and dollop the potatoes on top. Dot some butter over the potatoes and bake for about 20 minutes or until the potatoes are lightly browned. Serve with peas.

Serves 4

Goan shrimp curry

1 tablespoon vegetable oil
2 tablespoons curry paste
1 onion, finely chopped
2 tomatoes, chopped
3 garlic cloves, chopped
2 green chilies, finely chopped
1/2-in. piece ginger, grated
2 tablespoons tamarind puree
1/3 cup coconut milk
about 20 shrimp, peeled and
   deveined

Heat the oil in a deep frying pan and fry the curry paste for about a minute, by which time it should become aromatic. Add the onion and fry until it is golden. Add the tomato, garlic, green chili, and ginger and fry over low heat, stirring occasionally, for about 10 minutes or until the oil separates from the sauce.

Add the tamarind to the pan and bring to a boil. Add the coconut milk and stir. Season with salt.

Add the shrimp and bring slowly to a boil. (The sauce is not very liquidy, but it needs to be made very hot in order to cook the shrimp.) Simmer the shrimp for 3–5 minutes or until they turn bright pink all over. Stir them as they cook. Serve with rice or Indian bread.

Serves 4

Pulao with fried onions and spiced chicken

4 cups chicken stock
4 tablespoons vegetable oil
6 cardamom pods
2 (2-in.) pieces cinnamon stick
3 cloves
8 black peppercorns, crushed
1⅓ cups basmati rice
2 handfuls cilantro leaves
1 large onion, finely sliced
2 teaspoons curry paste
1 tablespoon tomato paste
2 tablespoons yogurt
2 skinless chicken breast fillets, cut
  into strips
yogurt, extra, to serve
mango chutney, to serve

Heat the chicken stock in a small saucepan until it is simmering. Heat 1 tablespoon of the oil over medium heat in a large, heavy-bottomed saucepan. Add the cardamom pods, cinnamon stick, cloves, and crushed peppercorns and fry for a minute. Reduce the heat to low, add the rice, and stir constantly for 1 minute. Add the heated stock and some salt to the rice and quickly bring everything to a boil. Cover the saucepan and simmer the rice over a low heat for 15 minutes. Leave the rice to stand for 10 minutes, then stir in the cilantro.

Heat 2 tablespoons of the oil in a frying pan and fry the onion until it is very soft. Increase the heat and keep frying until the onion turns dark brown. Drain the onion on paper towels, then add it to the rice.

Mix the curry paste, tomato paste, and yogurt together, then mix the paste thoroughly with the chicken strips.

Heat the remaining oil in a frying pan. Cook the chicken for about 4 minutes over a high heat until almost black in patches.

Serve the rice with the chicken strips, yogurt, and mango chutney.

Serves 4

Roast chicken pieces with herbed cheese

3/4 cup herbed cream cheese
1 teaspoon grated lemon zest
4 whole chicken legs or breasts,
  skin left on
2 leeks, cut into chunks
2 parsnips, cut into chunks
2 teaspoons olive oil

Preheat the oven to 400°F. Mix the cream cheese with the lemon zest. Loosen the skin from the whole legs or chicken breasts and spread 2 tablespoons of the cream cheese between the skin and flesh on each. Press the skin back down and season with salt and pepper.

Bring a saucepan of water to a boil and cook the leeks and parsnips for 4 minutes. Drain them well and put them in a single layer in a baking dish. Drizzle with the oil and season well. Put the chicken on top and put in the oven.

Roast for 40 minutes, by which time the skin should be browned and the cream cheese should have oozed out to form a sauce over the vegetables. Check that the vegetables are cooked and tender by prodding them with a knife. If they need to be cooked a little longer, cover the dish with foil and cook for another 5 minutes. Keep the chicken warm under foil.

Serves 4

Farfalle with shrimp and lemon horseradish cream

14 oz. farfalle pasta
1 tablespoon olive oil
2 shallots, sliced
about 32 shrimp, peeled and
  deveined
2 tablespoons lemon juice
6 tablespoons cream
2 teaspoons grated lemon zest
2 tablespoons horseradish cream
2 tablespoons chervil leaves

Cook the farfalle in a large saucepan of boiling salted water until al dente, stirring once or twice to make sure the pieces are not stuck together.

Heat the oil in a frying pan and add the shallots. Cook for a minute, then add the shrimp. Cook over high heat for 2–3 minutes or until the shrimp have turned bright pink and are cooked through. Add the lemon juice and toss well. Turn off the heat and leave everything in the pan.

Put the cream in a glass bowl and whisk until it just starts to thicken. Don't make it too thick; when you add the lemon zest and lemony shrimp the acid will thicken it further. Fold the lemon zest, horseradish cream, and chervil into the cream.

Drain the farfalle and pour it into a large bowl. Add the shrimp and any lemon juice to the bowl, then add the cream mixture. Fold together and season with salt and pepper.

Serves 4

Spaghetti bolognese

2 tablespoons olive oil
2 garlic cloves, crushed
1 large onion, chopped
1 carrot, finely chopped
1 celery stalk, finely chopped
1 lb. 2 oz. lean ground beef
2 cups beef stock
1½ cups red wine
2 (15-oz.) cans chopped tomatoes
1 teaspoon sugar
3 tablespoons finely chopped Italian
  parsley
1 lb. 2 oz. spaghetti
grated Parmesan cheese, to serve

Heat the olive oil in a large, deep frying pan, then add the garlic, onion, carrot, and celery and stir over low heat for 5 minutes until the vegetables are just starting to become tender.

Increase the heat before adding the beef. You'll need to stir the meat to break up any lumps—a wooden spoon is good for this. Once the meat is nicely browned, add the stock, wine, tomatoes, sugar, and parsley. Bring to a boil, then reduce the heat and simmer for about 1½ hours, stirring occasionally. Season with salt and freshly ground black pepper.

Shortly before serving, cook the spaghetti in a large saucepan of boiling water until al dente. Drain and serve with the meat sauce and the Parmesan cheese.

Serves 4–6

Spicy eggplant spaghetti

10½ oz. spaghetti
½ cup extra-virgin olive oil
2 red chilies, finely sliced
1 onion, finely chopped
3 garlic cloves, crushed
4 slices bacon, chopped
14 oz. eggplant, diced
2 tablespoons balsamic vinegar
2 tomatoes, chopped
3 tablespoons shredded basil

Cook the pasta in a large pan of rapidly boiling water until al dente, then drain.

Heat 1 tablespoon of the oil in a large, deep frying pan and cook the chili, onion, garlic, and bacon over medium heat for 5 minutes or until the onion is golden and the bacon browned. Remove from the pan and set aside.

Add half the remaining oil to the pan and cook half the eggplant over high heat, tossing to brown on all sides. Remove and repeat with the remaining oil and eggplant. Return the bacon mixture and all the eggplant to the pan, add the vinegar, tomato, and basil, and cook until heated through. Season well with salt and pepper.

Serve the spaghetti topped with the eggplant mixture.

Serves 4

Red beans and rice

1 cup red kidney beans
2 tablespoons vegetable oil
1 onion, finely chopped
1 green bell pepper, chopped
3 celery stalks, finely chopped
2 garlic cloves, crushed
8 oz. andouille or other spicy
  sausage, cut into pieces
2 ham hocks
2 bay leaves
1 cup long-grain rice
5 scallions, finely sliced, to garnish

Soak the red kidney beans overnight in cold water. Drain and put into a saucepan with enough cold water to cover the beans. Bring to a boil, then reduce the heat to a simmer.

Heat the oil in a frying pan and sauté the onion, pepper, celery, and garlic until soft. Add the sausage and sauté until it begins to brown around the edges.

Add the sautéed vegetables and sausage to the beans along with the ham and bay leaves. Bring to a boil, then reduce to a simmer and cook for 2½–3 hours, adding more water if necessary—the beans should be saucy but not too liquidy. When the beans are almost done, cook the rice in a separate saucepan until it is tender.

Top the cooked rice with the red kidney beans. Tear some meat off the ham hocks and add to each serving plate. Garnish with the sliced scallions.

Serves 4

Spaghetti with meatballs

Meatballs
1 lb. 2 oz. ground beef
1/2 cup fresh bread crumbs
1 onion, finely chopped
2 garlic cloves, crushed
2 teaspoons Worcestershire sauce
1 teaspoon dried oregano
1/4 cup all-purpose flour
2 tablespoons olive oil

Sauce
2 (14-oz.) cans chopped tomatoes
1 tablespoon olive oil
1 onion, finely chopped
2 garlic cloves, crushed
2 tablespoons tomato paste
1/2 cup beef stock
2 teaspoons sugar

1 lb. 2 oz. spaghetti
grated Parmesan cheese, to serve
  (optional)

Combine the beef, bread crumbs, onion, garlic, Worcestershire sauce, and oregano in a bowl and season to taste. Use your hands to mix the ingredients together well. Roll level tablespoons of the mixture into balls, dust lightly with the flour, and shake off the excess. Heat the oil in a deep frying pan and cook the meatballs in batches, turning frequently, until browned all over. Drain well.

To make the sauce, puree the tomatoes in a food processor or blender. Heat the oil in the cleaned frying pan. Add the onion and cook over medium heat for a few minutes until soft and just lightly golden. Add the garlic and cook for 1 minute more. Add the pureed tomatoes, tomato paste, stock, and sugar to the pan and stir to combine. Bring the mixture to a boil and add the meatballs. Reduce the heat and simmer for 15 minutes, turning the meatballs once. Season with salt and pepper.

Meanwhile, cook the spaghetti in a large pan of boiling water until just tender. Drain, divide among serving plates, and top with the meatballs and sauce. Serve with grated Parmesan if desired.

Serves 4

Beef Stroganoff

1 lb. 2 oz. rump steak
2 tablespoons all-purpose flour
2 tablespoons olive oil
1 onion, finely chopped
1 garlic clove, crushed
4 cups button mushrooms, sliced
1 tablespoon tomato paste
1 1/4 cups sour cream
finely chopped parsley, to serve

Trim excess fat off the meat and slice it across the grain into thin pieces. Put the flour in a plastic bag and season well with salt and cracked black pepper. Add the steak and shake to coat the meat. Shake off any excess flour.

Heat 1 tablespoon oil in a large, heavy-bottomed frying pan over high heat. Add the meat and cook in batches until well browned. Remove from the pan and set aside.

Heat the remaining oil and add the onion. Cook for 2–3 minutes, or until soft and translucent, then add the garlic and stir briefly. Add the mushrooms and cook for about 3 minutes or until soft. Stir in the tomato paste and sour cream, then add the beef strips. Stir until well combined and heated through. Sprinkle with chopped parsley before serving with rice.

Serves 4

Snapper pies

2 tablespoons olive oil
4 onions, thinly sliced
1½ cups fish stock
3½ cups cream
2 lb. 4 oz. skinless snapper fillets, cut
  into large pieces
2 sheets puff pastry, thawed
1 egg, lightly beaten

Preheat the oven to 425°F. Heat the oil in a deep frying pan, add the onions, and stir over medium heat for 20 minutes or until the onion is slightly caramelized. Add the fish stock, bring to a boil, and cook for 10 minutes or until the liquid is nearly evaporated. Stir in the cream and bring to a boil. Reduce the heat and simmer for 20 minutes or until the liquid is reduced by half.

Divide half the sauce among four 2-cup ramekins. Place some fish pieces in each ramekin and top with the remaining sauce. Cut the pastry sheets slightly larger than the tops of the ramekins. Brush the edges of the pastry with a little of the egg, press the pastry onto the ramekins, and brush the pastry top with the remaining beaten egg. Bake for 30 minutes or until well puffed.

Serves 4

Osso buco with gremolata

2 tablespoons olive oil
1 onion, finely chopped
1 garlic clove, crushed
2 lb. 4 oz. veal shin slices (osso buco)
2 tablespoons all-purpose flour
14-oz. can tomatoes, roughly
  chopped
1 cup white wine
1 cup chicken stock

Gremolata
2 tablespoons finely chopped Italian
  parsley
2 teaspoons grated lemon zest
1 teaspoon finely chopped garlic

Heat 1 tablespoon oil in a large, shallow, flameproof casserole dish. Add the onion and cook over low heat until soft and golden. Add the garlic. Cook for 1 minute, then remove from the dish.

Heat the remaining oil and brown the veal in batches, then remove. Return the onion to the casserole and stir in the flour. Cook for 30 seconds and remove from the heat. Slowly stir in the tomatoes, wine, and stock, combining well with the flour. Return the veal to the casserole.

Return to the heat and bring to a boil, stirring. Cover and reduce the heat to low so that it is just simmering. Cook for $2\frac{1}{2}$ hours or until the meat is very tender and almost falling off the bones.

To make the gremolata, combine the parsley, lemon zest, and garlic in a bowl. When the osso buco is ready, sprinkle the gremolata over the top and serve with risotto or plain rice.

Serves 4

Note: Try to make this a day in advance, as the flavors will improve considerably.

Asian chicken noodle soup

3 dried Chinese mushrooms
6½ oz. thin dry egg noodles
1 tablespoon vegetable oil
4 scallions, julienned
1 tablespoon soy sauce
2 tablespoons rice wine, mirin, or
    sherry
5 cups chicken stock
½ small barbecued chicken,
    shredded
1¾ oz. sliced ham, cut into strips
1 cup bean sprouts
cilantro leaves, to garnish
thinly sliced red chilies, to garnish

Soak the mushrooms in boiling water for 10 minutes to soften them. Squeeze dry, then remove the tough stems from the mushrooms and slice them thinly.

Cook the noodles in a large pan of boiling water for 3 minutes, or according to the manufacturer's directions. Drain and cut the noodles into shorter lengths with scissors.

Heat the oil in a large, heavy-bottomed pan. Add the mushrooms and scallions. Cook for 1 minute, then add the soy sauce, rice wine, and stock. Bring slowly to a boil and cook for 1 minute. Reduce the heat, then add the noodles, shredded chicken, ham, and bean sprouts. Heat through for 2 minutes without allowing to boil.

Use tongs to divide the noodles among four bowls, ladle in the remaining mixture, and garnish with cilantro leaves and sliced chilies.

Serves 4

Genovese pesto sauce

Pesto
2 garlic cloves
1/2 cup pine nuts
medium bunch basil, stems removed
3/4 cup extra-virgin olive oil
1 3/4 oz. Parmesan cheese, finely
  grated, plus extra to serve

1 lb. 2 oz. trenette pasta
1 cup green beans, trimmed
6 oz. (about 2) small potatoes, very
  thinly sliced

Put the garlic and pine nuts in a mortar and pestle or food processor and pound or process until finely ground. Add the basil and then drizzle in the olive oil a little at a time while pounding or processing. When you have a thick puree, stop adding the oil. Season and mix in the Parmesan.

Bring a large saucepan of salted water to a boil. Add the pasta, green beans, and potatoes, stirring well to prevent the pasta from sticking together. Cook until the pasta is al dente (the vegetables should be cooked by this time), then drain, reserving a little of the water.

Return the pasta and vegetables to the saucepan, add the pesto, and mix well. If necessary, add some of the reserved water to loosen the pasta. Season and serve immediately with the extra Parmesan.

Serves 4

Shrimp pulao

1 cup basmati rice
10½ oz. small shrimp
3 tablespoons vegetable oil
1 onion, finely chopped
1 stick of cinnamon
6 cardamom pods
5 cloves
1 stalk lemongrass, finely chopped
4 garlic cloves, crushed
2-in. piece of fresh ginger, grated
¼ teaspoon ground turmeric

Wash the rice under cold running water and drain. Peel and devein the shrimp, then wash and pat dry with paper towels.

Heat the oil in a frying pan over a low heat and fry the onion, spices, and lemongrass. Stir in the garlic, ginger, and turmeric. Add the shrimp and stir until pink. Toss in the rice and fry for 2 minutes. Pour in 2 cups of boiling water and add a pinch of salt. Bring to a boil. Reduce the heat and simmer for 15 minutes. Remove from the heat, cover, and let stand for 10 minutes. Fluff up the rice before serving.

Serves 4

Spicy Portuguese chicken soup

10 cups chicken stock
1 onion, cut into thin wedges
1 celery stalk, finely chopped
1 teaspoon grated lemon zest
3 tomatoes, peeled, seeded, and
   chopped
1 sprig mint
1 tablespoon olive oil
2 chicken breast fillets
1 cup long-grain rice
2 tablespoons lemon juice
2 tablespoons shredded mint

Combine the chicken stock, onion, celery, lemon zest, tomatoes, mint, and olive oil in a large saucepan. Slowly bring to a boil, then reduce the heat, add the chicken, and simmer gently for 20–25 minutes or until the chicken is cooked through.

Remove the chicken from the saucepan and discard the mint sprig. Allow the chicken to cool, then slice thinly.

Meanwhile, add the rice to the pan and simmer for 25–30 minutes or until the rice is tender. Return the sliced chicken to the pan, add the lemon juice, and stir for 1–2 minutes or until the chicken is warmed through. Season with salt and pepper and stir in the shredded mint.

Serves 6

Spiced eggplant

2 eggplants, sliced
2 onions, finely chopped
3/4-in. piece fresh ginger, grated
4 garlic cloves, crushed
2 red chilies, finely chopped
2 cups canned tomatoes
vegetable oil, for frying
1/2 teaspoon ground turmeric
1/2 teaspoon black onion seeds
2 teaspoons garam masala
large handful of cilantro, chopped

Put the eggplant slices in a colander, sprinkle them with salt, and let stand for 30 minutes. Rinse the slices and squeeze to get rid of any excess water, then pat dry with paper towels.

Finely chop the tomatoes, then mix the onion, ginger, garlic, and chili with the tomatoes.

Heat a little oil in a large, deep, heavy-bottomed frying pan. When it is hot, add as many eggplant slices as you can fit in a single layer. Cook them over a medium heat until they are browned on both sides, then drain them to get rid of any excess oil. Cook the rest of the eggplant in batches, using as much oil as you need and draining off the excess.

Heat a tablespoon of oil in the frying pan, add the turmeric, black onion seeds, and garam masala and stir for a few seconds, then add the tomato mixture. Cook, stirring for 5 minutes or until the mixture thickens. Carefully add the cooked eggplant so the slices stay whole, cover the pan, and cook gently for about 15 minutes. Season with salt to taste and stir in the cilantro.

Serves 4

Fajitas

3/4 cup olive oil
2 tablespoons lime juice
4 garlic cloves, chopped
3 red chilies, chopped
2 tablespoons tequila (optional)
2 lb. 4 oz. rump steak, thinly sliced
  into strips
1 red bell pepper, thinly sliced
1 yellow bell pepper, thinly sliced
1 red onion, thinly sliced
8 flour tortillas
guacamole, to serve
shredded lettuce, to serve
diced tomatoes, to serve
sour cream, to serve

Make a marinade out of the oil, lime juice, garlic, chilies, tequila, and some black pepper. Add the meat, cover, and marinate it for several hours or overnight.

Drain the meat and toss it with the bell peppers and onion. Around the time that you want to eat, wrap the tortillas in foil and warm them in a 300°F oven for about 5 minutes. Cook the meat and vegetables in batches in a sizzling-hot, heavy-bottomed frying pan until cooked, then scoop onto a serving plate and put in the middle of the table with the tortillas, guacamole, shredded lettuce, diced tomatoes, and sour cream. Let everybody assemble their own fajitas.

Serves 4

Dinner

Twice-baked cheese soufflés

1 cup milk
3 black peppercorns
1 onion, cut in half and studded
   with 2 cloves
1 bay leaf
5 1/2 tablespoons butter
1/2 cup self-rising flour
2 eggs, separated
4 1/2 oz. Gruyère cheese, grated
1 cup cream
1/2 cup Parmesan cheese, finely
   grated
salad, to serve

Preheat the oven to 350°F. Lightly grease four 1/2-cup ramekins. Place the milk, peppercorns, onion, and bay leaf in a saucepan and heat until nearly boiling. Remove from the heat and let it infuse for 10 minutes. Strain.

Melt the butter in a saucepan, add the flour, and cook over medium heat for 1 minute. Remove from the heat and gradually stir in the infused milk, then return to the heat and stir until the mixture boils and thickens. Simmer for 1 minute.

Transfer the mixture to a bowl and add the egg yolks and Gruyère cheese. Beat the egg whites until soft peaks form, then gently fold into the cheese sauce. Divide the mixture between the ramekins and place in a baking dish half-filled with hot water. Bake for 15 minutes. Remove from the baking dish, cool, and refrigerate.

Preheat the oven to 400°F. Remove the soufflés from the ramekins and place on ovenproof plates. Pour cream on them and sprinkle with Parmesan. Bake for 20 minutes or until puffed and golden. Serve with a salad.

Serves 4

Pork loin with pickled eggplant

2 (1 lb. 2 oz.) pieces pork loin fillet
2 tablespoons hoisin sauce
large pinch of five-spice powder
4 tablespoons vegetable oil
1 eggplant, cut into wedges
2 tablespoons soy sauce
2 teaspoons sesame oil
2 tablespoons balsamic vinegar
¼ teaspoon superfine sugar
2 bok choy, cut into quarters

Put the pork in a dish and add the hoisin sauce, five-spice powder, and a tablespoon of oil. Rub the mixture over the pork and set it to one side. Heat another 2 tablespoons of oil in a nonstick frying pan and add the eggplant. Fry it until it softens and starts to brown, then add the soy sauce, sesame oil, vinegar, and sugar and toss for a minute. Slide the eggplant onto a plate and wipe out the frying pan.

Put the remaining oil in the frying pan and put it over medium heat. Add the pork and fry it on all sides until it is browned and cooked through. The time this takes will depend on how thick your piece of pork is — when it is cooked, it will feel firm when pressed. Put the eggplant back in the pan to heat through.

Remove the pork and let stand for a minute or two. Cook the bok choy in a saucepan with a little bit of boiling water for 1 minute, then drain well. Slice the pork into medallions and serve it with the pickled eggplant and bok choy.

Serves 4

Coq au vin

1 tablespoon olive oil
12 white pearl onions, peeled
3 slices bacon, chopped
3 tablespoons butter
3 lb. 5 oz. chicken pieces
2 garlic cloves, crushed
1½ cups dry red wine
2 tablespoons brandy
1 tablespoon chopped thyme
1 bay leaf
4 parsley stalks
2½ cups button mushrooms, halved
1 tablespoon butter, extra, softened
1 tablespoon all-purpose flour
chopped Italian parsley, to serve

Preheat the oven to 325°F. Heat the oil in a large, heavy-bottomed frying pan and add the onions. Cook until browned, then add the bacon and cook until browned. Remove the bacon and onions and add the butter to the pan. When the butter is foaming, add the chicken in a single layer and cook in batches until well browned. Transfer the chicken to an ovenproof dish, draining it of any fat, then add the onions and bacon.

Pour any excess fat out of the frying pan and add the garlic, wine, brandy, thyme, bay leaf, and parsley stalks. Bring to a boil and pour over the chicken. Cook, covered, in the oven for 1 hour and 25 minutes, then add the mushrooms and cook for 30 minutes. Drain through a colander and reserve the liquid in a pan. Keep the chicken warm in the oven.

Mix the softened butter and flour together, bring the liquid in the pan to a boil, and whisk in the flour-and-butter paste in two batches, then reduce the heat and simmer until the liquid thickens slightly. Remove the parsley and bay leaf from the chicken and return the chicken to the ovenproof dish. Pour in the sauce, sprinkle with chopped parsley, and serve.

Serves 4

Beef Wellington

2 lb. 12 oz. piece of rib eye steak, trimmed
1 tablespoon vegetable oil
4 1/2 oz. pâté
1/2 cup button mushrooms, sliced
13-oz. block of puff pastry, thawed
1 egg, lightly beaten
1 sheet puff pastry, extra, thawed
green beans, to serve
rosemary, to garnish

Preheat the oven to 415°F. To help the beef keep its shape, tie it four or five times along its length, then rub with pepper. Heat the oil over high heat in a large, heavy-bottomed pan, then cook the meat until it is browned all over. Take the beef out of the pan and let it cool, then cut off the string. Smear the pâté over the top and sides of the beef, then use this as glue to stick the mushrooms on.

The idea is to enclose the beef in puff pastry. Start by rolling the block of pastry out on a lightly floured surface until it is big enough. Then place the beef on the pastry, brush the edges with egg, and bring the edges up until you have a package. Use some more of the beaten egg to seal the package, then neatly fold in the ends. Lift the beef onto a greased baking tray so the seam is underneath.

Cut decorative shapes from the extra sheet of pastry. Use the egg to stick the shapes on, then brush the Wellington all over with more of the egg. Cut a few slits in the top to allow the steam to escape. Bake for 45 minutes for rare, 1 hour for medium, or 1 1/2 hours for well done. Rest for 10 minutes, then slice and serve. Serve with green beans and garnish with rosemary.

Serves 6–8

Swordfish with anchovy and caper sauce

Sauce
1 large garlic clove
1 tablespoon capers, rinsed and finely
   chopped
1 3/4 oz. anchovy fillets, finely chopped
1 tablespoon finely chopped rosemary
   or dried oregano
finely grated zest and juice of
   1/2 lemon
4 tablespoons extra-virgin olive oil
1 large tomato, finely chopped

4 swordfish steaks
1 tablespoon extra-virgin olive oil
crusty Italian bread, to serve

Put the garlic in a mortar and pestle with a little salt and crush it. To make the sauce, mix together the garlic, capers, anchovies, rosemary or oregano, lemon zest and juice, oil, and tomato. Let stand for 10 minutes.

Preheat a broiler to very hot. Using paper towels, pat the swordfish dry and lightly brush with the olive oil. Season with salt and pepper. Sear the swordfish over high heat for about 2 minutes on each side (depending on the thickness of the steaks) or until just cooked. The best way to check if the fish is cooked is to pull apart the center of one steak—the flesh should be opaque. (Serve with the cut side underneath.)

If the cooked swordfish is a little oily, drain it on paper towels, then place on serving plates and drizzle with the sauce. Serve with Italian bread to mop up the sauce.

Serves 4

Pepper steak

4 (7-oz.) fillet steaks
2 tablespoons vegetable oil
6 tablespoons black peppercorns,
   crushed
3 tablespoons butter
3 tablespoons Cognac or brandy
½ cup heavy cream
green salad, to serve

Rub the steaks on both sides with the oil and press the crushed peppercorns into the meat so they don't come off while frying. Melt the butter in a large frying pan and cook the steaks for 2–4 minutes on each side, depending on how you like your steak.

Add the Cognac or brandy and flambé by lighting the pan with your gas flame or a match (stand well back when you do this and keep a pan lid handy for emergencies). Lift the steaks out onto a warm plate. Add the wine to the pan and boil, stirring, for 1 minute to deglaze the pan. Add the cream and stir for a couple of minutes. Season with salt and pepper and pour over the steaks. Serve with green salad.

Serves 4

Teppanyaki

12-oz. fillet steak
assorted vegetables, such as
    green beans, eggplant, shiitake
    mushrooms, red or green bell
    pepper, and scallions
12 shrimp, peeled and deveined,
    tails intact
3 tablespoons vegetable oil
soy sauce
rice, to serve

Slice the meat very thinly. The secret to this is to partially freeze the meat (about 30 minutes should be enough), then slice it with a very sharp knife. Place the meat slices in a single layer on a large serving platter and season well with salt and pepper.

Cut the vegetables into long, thin strips, then arrange them in separate bundles on a plate. Arrange the shrimp on a third plate.

The idea of teppanyaki is to cook the meal at the table on a very hot electric grill or frying pan. Lightly brush the pan with the oil. Quickly fry about a quarter of the meat, searing on both sides, and then push it over to the edge of the pan while you cook about a quarter of the vegetables and the shrimp. Serve a small portion of the meat and vegetables to the diners, who then dip the food into soy sauce. Repeat the process with the remaining meat and vegetables, cooking in batches as extra helpings are required. Serve with rice.

Serves 4

Steak with green peppercorn sauce

4 (7-oz.) tenderloin steaks
2 tablespoons butter
2 teaspoons vegetable oil
1 cup beef stock
3/4 cup whipping cream
2 teaspoons cornstarch
2 tablespoons green peppercorns in
   brine, rinsed and drained
2 tablespoons brandy
French fries, to serve
rosemary, to garnish

Bash the steaks with a meat mallet to 1/2 inch thick. Next, nick the edges of the steaks to prevent them from curling when they are cooking.

Heat the butter and oil in a large, heavy-bottomed frying pan over high heat. Fry the steaks for 2–4 minutes on each side, depending on how you like your steak. Transfer to a serving plate and cover with foil.

Add the stock to the pan juices and stir over low heat until boiling. Combine the cream and cornstarch, then pour the mixture into the pan and stir constantly until the sauce becomes smooth and thick—a few minutes will do the trick. Add the peppercorns and brandy and boil for 1 more minute before taking the pan off the heat. Spoon the sauce over the steaks. Serve with French fries and garnish with rosemary.

Serves 4

Pork chops pizzaiola

4 pork chops
4 tablespoons olive oil
1 lb. 5 oz. (about 4 medium) ripe
    tomatoes
3 garlic cloves, crushed
3 basil leaves, torn into pieces
1 teaspoon finely chopped Italian
    parsley, to serve

Using scissors or a knife, cut the pork fat at $1/4$-in. intervals around the rind. Brush the chops with 1 tablespoon of the olive oil and season well with salt and pepper.

Remove the stems from the tomatoes and score a cross in the bottom of each one. Blanch in boiling water for 30 seconds. Transfer to cold water, peel the skin away from the cross, and chop the tomatoes.

Heat 2 tablespoons of the oil in a saucepan over low heat and add the garlic. Soften without browning for 1–2 minutes, then add the tomatoes and season. Increase the heat, bring to a boil, and cook for 5 minutes or until thick. Stir in the basil.

Heat the remaining oil in a large frying pan with a tight-fitting lid. Brown the chops in batches over medium–high heat for 2 minutes on each side. Place in a slightly overlapping row down the center of the pan and spoon the sauce over the top, covering the chops completely. Cover the pan and cook over low heat for about 5 minutes. Sprinkle with parsley to serve.

Serves 4

Baked sea bass with wild rice stuffing

2 small fennel bulbs
1/3 cup wild rice
1 cup fish stock
2 tablespoons butter
2 tablespoons olive oil
1 onion, chopped
1 garlic clove, crushed
grated zest of 1 lemon
4 lb. 8 oz. sea bass, bass, or any
  large white fish, gutted and scaled
extra-virgin olive oil
1 lemon, quartered
2 teaspoons chopped oregano
lemon wedges, to serve

Preheat the oven to 375°F and lightly grease a large, shallow, ovenproof dish. Finely slice the fennel, reserving the green fronds.

Put the wild rice and stock in a saucepan with 3 tablespoons of water and bring to a boil. Simmer for 30 minutes or until tender, then drain. Heat the butter and olive oil in a large frying pan and gently cook the fennel, onion, and garlic for 12–15 minutes or until softened but not browned. Add the lemon zest, stir in the rice, and season with salt and pepper.

Put the fish on a cutting board. Stuff the fish with a heaping tablespoon of the fennel mixture and a quarter of the reserved fennel fronds. Transfer to an ovenproof dish. Brush with extra-virgin olive oil, squeeze the lemon on top, and season well.

Spoon the remainder of the cooked fennel into the ovenproof dish and sprinkle with half the oregano. Put the fish on top of the fennel. Sprinkle the remaining oregano over the fish and loosely cover the dish with foil. Bake for 25 minutes or until it is just cooked through. Serve with lemon wedges.

Serves 4

Braised sausages with Puy lentils

1 tablespoon olive oil
4 oz. pancetta, cubed
2 red onions, finely chopped
12 Toulouse or pork sausages
2 garlic cloves, peeled and smashed
2 sprigs thyme leaves
1⅓ cups Puy lentils
3 cups chicken stock
10½ oz. spinach leaves, finely
  chopped
⅓ cup crème fraîche

Heat the oil in a wide, heavy-bottomed frying pan with a lid and fry the pancetta until it is browned. Take it out using a slotted spoon, and put it in a bowl. Put the onion in the pan and cook until it is soft and only lightly browned. Take the onion out and add it to the pancetta. Put the sausages in the same pan and fry them until they are very brown all over. Put the pancetta and onion back in with the sausages.

Add the garlic and the thyme leaves to the frying pan along with the lentils and mix together. Add the stock and bring to a boil. Put a lid on the frying pan and slowly simmer the mixture for 30–35 minutes or until the lentils are tender. Stir the spinach through.

Season the lentils with salt and pepper and stir in the crème fraîche. Serve the sausages with the lentils in shallow bowls. Serve with bread.

Serves 4

Salmon nori roll with sesame noodles

10½ oz. soba noodles
1½ teaspoons sesame oil
2 tablespoons sesame seeds
2 pieces salmon fillet, bones removed
2 sheets nori
1 tablespoon butter
9 oz. spinach leaves

Cook the noodles in a large saucepan of boiling salted water for about 5 minutes or until they are just cooked. The cooking time will vary depending on the brand of noodles. Drain the noodles, add the sesame oil and some seasoning, then toss them so they are coated in the oil. Dry-fry the sesame seeds in a frying pan until they start to color and smell toasted, then add them to the noodles. Cover and keep warm.

Cut each salmon fillet in half horizontally and trim the edges. Cut each sheet of nori in half with a pair of scissors and lay a piece of salmon fillet on top of each half. Season well, then roll up the fillets to make neat log shapes. Trim off any bits of nori or salmon that stick out. Using a sharp knife, cut each roll into three pieces.

Heat the butter in a nonstick frying pan and fry the pieces of roll until they are golden on each side and almost cooked all the way through. This will take about 4 minutes on each side. Lift out the rolls. Add the spinach to the pan, stir it until it wilts, then turn off the heat. Serve the salmon with the noodles and some spinach on the side.

Serves 4

Lamb shanks with chickpeas

1 tablespoon vegetable oil
4 large or 8 small lamb shanks
2 onions, finely chopped
2 garlic cloves, crushed
1 tablespoon harissa
1 cinnamon stick
2 (14-oz.) cans chopped tomatoes
2 (10½-oz.) cans chickpeas, drained
½ cup green olives
½ tablespoon preserved lemon or
  lemon zest, finely chopped
2 tablespoons mint, chopped

Heat the oil in a large casserole dish over a medium heat and fry the lamb shanks until they are well browned all over. Add the onion and garlic and fry them for a couple of minutes until the onion starts to soften.

Add the harissa, cinnamon, and salt and pepper to the casserole, stir together, then add the chopped tomatoes and bring to a boil. If there doesn't seem to be enough liquid (the shanks should be pretty well covered), add a bit of water. Put the lid on and turn the heat down until the liquid is simmering, then cook for 50 minutes.

Add the chickpeas, olives, and lemon to the pan and stir them into the liquid. Season to taste and continue cooking with the lid off for another 20 to 30 minutes. By this time, the lamb should be very tender and almost falling off the bone. If it isn't, just keep cooking, checking every 5 minutes. Using a big spoon, scoop any orange-colored oil from the top, then stir in the mint. Serve with extra harissa if you would like the sauce a little hotter.

Serves 4

Grilled trout with lemon butter and couscous

1 cup instant couscous
1 tablespoon olive oil
1 onion, finely chopped
4 pieces red or yellow bell pepper,
   roasted and chopped
small handful of pine nuts
lemon juice and zest from 2 lemons
large handful of mint, chopped
4 rainbow trout fillets, skin removed
2 tablespoons butter, softened

Preheat the broiler. Bring 2 cups water to a boil in a saucepan and add the couscous. Take the pan off the heat and let stand for 10 minutes.

Heat the oil in a frying pan and fry the onion until it is lightly browned. Add the bell peppers and pine nuts, then stir in the couscous. Stir in half of the lemon juice and zest, along with the mint.

Put the trout fillets on an oiled baking pan. Mix the butter with the rest of the lemon zest and spread it on the fish. Grill the fish for 6 minutes or until it is just cooked through. Sprinkle on the rest of the lemon juice and season well.

Serve the trout (take it off the pan carefully, as it doesn't have any skin to hold it together) on the couscous with any buttery juices poured over it.

Serves 4

Lamb cutlets with onion marmalade

2 tablespoons butter
⅓ cup olive oil
4 onions, finely sliced
2 teaspoons brown sugar
2 teaspoons thyme leaves
2 tablespoons parsley, finely chopped
12 French-trimmed lamb chops
2 tablespoons lemon juice

Heat the butter and half the olive oil together in a saucepan. Add the onion, sugar, and thyme and stir well. Turn the heat to low, cover the saucepan, and cook the onion, stirring it occasionally for 30–35 minutes or until it is very soft and golden. Season well, stir in the parsley, and keep it warm over a very low heat.

Heat the remaining oil in a frying pan or brush a griddle with oil and, when it is hot, add the lamb chops in a single layer. Fry for 2 minutes on each side or until the lamb is browned on the outside but still feels springy when you press it. Add the lemon juice and season well.

Put a small pile of the onion and herb marmalade on each plate and place the lamb chops around it.

Serves 4

Summer seafood marinara

10½ oz. fresh saffron angel-hair pasta
1 tablespoon extra-virgin olive oil
2 tablespoons butter
2 garlic cloves, finely chopped
1 large onion, finely chopped
1 small red chili, finely chopped
1 lb. 5 oz. canned peeled tomatoes,
  chopped
1 cup white wine
zest of 1 lemon
½ tablespoon sugar
7 oz. scallops
1 lb. 2 oz. raw shrimp, peeled and
  deveined
10½ oz. clams, in the shell

Cook the pasta in a large saucepan
of rapidly boiling water until al dente.
Drain and keep warm.

Heat the oil and butter in a large frying
pan, add the garlic, onion, and chili,
and cook over a medium heat for
5 minutes or until soft but not golden.
Add the tomatoes and wine and bring
to a boil. Cook for 10 minutes or until
the sauce has reduced and thickened
slightly.

Add the lemon zest, sugar, scallops,
shrimp, and clams and cook,
covered, for 5 minutes or until the
seafood is tender. Discard any clams
that do not open. Season with salt
and pepper. Serve the sauce on top
of the pasta.

Serves 4

Beef cooked in Guinness with celeriac puree

2 tablespoons vegetable oil
2 lb. 4 oz. chuck steak, cubed
2 onions, chopped
1 garlic clove, crushed
2 teaspoons brown sugar
2 teaspoons all-purpose flour
1/2 cup Guinness stout
1 1/2 cups beef stock
1 bay leaf
2 sprigs thyme
1 celeriac
1 potato, cubed
1 cup milk
1 tablespoon butter
4 slices baguette, toasted
1 teaspoon Dijon mustard

Preheat the oven to 350°F. Heat half of the oil in a frying pan over high heat and fry the meat in batches until it is browned all over. Add more oil as needed. Put the meat in a flameproof casserole dish.

Add the onion to the frying pan and fry it gently over a low heat. When the onion starts to brown, add the garlic and brown sugar and cook until the onion is fairly brown. Stir in the flour, then transfer to the casserole dish.

Put the Guinness and stock in the frying pan and bring it to a boil, then pour into the casserole dish. Add the bay leaf and thyme to the casserole dish and season well. Bring to a boil, cover with a lid, and put the casserole in the oven for 2 hours.

Peel and chop the celeriac. Put the pieces into a bowl of water as you cut them. Put the potato and celeriac in a saucepan with the milk and bring to a boil. Cover and cook for 15 minutes, then mash together with the milk. Season well and add the butter.

Spread the bread with the mustard and serve with the beef ladled on top and the celeriac puree on the side.

Serves 4

Roast lamb

2 rosemary sprigs
3 garlic cloves
2½ oz. pancetta
4 lb. 8 oz. leg of lamb, shank bone
  cut off just above the joint, trimmed
  of excess fat, and tied
1 large onion
½ cup olive oil
1½ cups dry white wine

Preheat the oven to 450°F. Strip the leaves off the rosemary sprigs and chop them with the garlic and pancetta until pastelike. Season with salt and pepper.

With the point of a sharp knife, make incisions about ½ in. deep all over the lamb. Rub the rosemary filling over the surface of the lamb, pushing it into the incisions.

Cut the onion into four thick slices and put them in the center of a roasting pan. Place the lamb on top and gently pour the olive oil over it. Roast for 15 minutes. Reduce the oven temperature to 350°F and pour in 1 cup of the wine. Roast for 1½ hours for medium-rare, or longer if you prefer. Baste a couple of times and add a little water if the juices start to burn in the pan. Transfer the lamb to a carving platter and leave to rest for 10 minutes.

Remove the onion and spoon the excess fat from the pan. Place over high heat, pour in the remaining wine, and cook for 3–4 minutes or until the sauce reduces and thickens. Taste for seasoning. Slice the lamb and serve with the sauce spooned over it.

Serves 4

Pork chops with apples and cider

1 tablespoon vegetable oil
2 onions, sliced
2 Golden Delicious apples, cored and
  cut into wedges
2 teaspoons superfine sugar
2 teaspoons butter
4 thick pork chops, trimmed around
  the edges
$\frac{1}{3}$ cup cider
$\frac{1}{3}$ cup cream
roasted potatoes, to serve
green salad, to serve

Heat the oil in a large nonstick frying pan, add the onions, and fry for 5 minutes or until soft and just beginning to brown. Slide the onions out onto a plate.

Add the apple wedges to the pan and fry them for a minute or two—they should not break up, but should start to soften and brown. Add the sugar and butter and shake the pan until the apples start to caramelize. Transfer the apples to the plate with the onion.

Put the pork chops in the frying pan, add a bit of salt and pepper, and fry them for 4 minutes on each side or until they are cooked through. Put the onions and apples back in the pan and heat them, then add the cider and bring to a simmer. Once the liquid is bubbling, add the cream and shake the pan so everything mixes together. Let it bubble for a minute, then season well and serve with roasted potatoes and a green salad.

Serves 4

Thai mussels with noodles

4 lb. 8 oz. mussels
8½ oz. glass noodles
2 garlic cloves, crushed
2 scallions, finely chopped
2 tablespoons red curry paste
2/3 cup coconut cream
juice of 2 limes
2 tablespoons fish sauce
handful of cilantro leaves

Rinse the mussels in cold water and pull off any beards. Look at each one individually: if it isn't tightly closed, tap it on the work surface to see if it will close. Throw away any mussels that won't close.

Soak the noodles in boiling water for a minute or two. Drain them and, using a pair of scissors, cut them into shorter lengths.

Put the mussels in a deep frying pan or wok with the garlic and scallions and ½ cup water. Bring the water to a boil, then cover with a lid and cook the mussels for 2–3 minutes, shaking occasionally, until they are all open. Throw away any that don't open. Pour the whole lot, including any liquid, into a sieve lined with a piece of cheesecloth, reserving the liquid.

Pour the cooking liquid back into the pan, add the curry paste and coconut cream, and stir together. Bring the mixture to a boil, then add the lime juice and fish sauce. Put the mussels back in the pan. Cook for a minute, then stir in the cilantro leaves.

Put some noodles in each bowl and ladle the mussels on top.

Serves 4

Saltimbocca

8 small veal cutlets
8 slices prosciutto
8 sage leaves
2 tablespoons olive oil
4¹/₂ tablespoons butter
³/₄ cup dry Marsala or dry white wine

Place the veal between two sheets of waxed paper and pound with a meat mallet or rolling pin until they are ¹/₄ in. thick. Make sure you pound them evenly. Peel off the paper and season lightly with salt and pepper. Cut the prosciutto slices to the same size as the veal. Cover each piece of veal with a slice of prosciutto and place a sage leaf in the center. Secure the sage leaf with a toothpick.

Heat the olive oil and half the butter in a large frying pan. Add the veal in batches and fry, prosciutto side up, over medium heat for 3–4 minutes or until the veal is just cooked through. Briefly flip the saltimbocca over and fry the prosciutto side. Transfer each batch to a warm plate as it is done.

Pour off the oil from the pan and add the Marsala or wine. Bring to a boil and cook over high heat until reduced by half, scraping up the bits from the bottom of the pan. Add the remaining butter and, when it has melted, season the sauce. Remove the toothpicks and spoon the sauce over the veal to serve.

Serves 4

Steak with maître d'hotel butter

6½ tablespoons unsalted butter, softened
2 teaspoons finely chopped parsley
lemon juice
4 steaks, about ½ in. thick
1 tablespoon olive oil

Cream the butter in a bowl, using a wooden spoon, then beat in a pinch of salt, a pinch of pepper, and the parsley. Add about 2 teaspoons of lemon juice, a few drops at a time. Let the butter harden in the refrigerator a little, then form it into a log shape by rolling it up in waxed paper. Put it in the refrigerator until you need it.

Season the steaks with salt and pepper on both sides. Heat the oil in a large frying pan and, when it is very hot, add the steaks. Cook them for 2 minutes on each side for rare, 3 minutes on each side for medium, and 4 minutes on each side for well done. The cooking times may vary depending on the thickness of your steaks—if they are thin, give them a slightly shorter time and if they are thick, cook them for longer.

Cut the butter into slices and put a couple of slices on top of each steak. The heat of the steak will melt the butter. Serve with potatoes and vegetables or salad.

Serves 4

Corned beef with parsley sauce

3 lb. 5 oz. corned beef
1 teaspoon black peppercorns
5 cloves
2 bay leaves, torn
2 tablespoons brown sugar

Parsley sauce
3½ tablespoons butter
1½ tablespoons all-purpose flour
1¾ cups milk
½ cup beef stock
2 tablespoons chopped Italian parsley

Soak the corned beef in cold water for 45 minutes, changing the water three or four times. This helps eliminate some of the salty flavor.

Lift the beef out of the water and put it in a large, heavy-bottomed saucepan with the peppercorns, cloves, bay leaves, brown sugar, and enough cold water to just cover it. Bring to a boil, then reduce the heat to very low and simmer for 1½–1¾ hours. Turn the meat over every half hour and keep an eye on the water level—you'll probably need to add some more. You don't want the water to boil or the meat will become tough, so use a heat diffuser mat if you need to. Remove the meat from the pan and let it rest for 15 minutes.

To make the parsley sauce, melt the butter in a saucepan over medium heat, then stir in the flour and keep stirring for 1 minute. Take the pan off the heat and pour in the milk and stock, whisking until smooth. Return the pan to the heat and cook, whisking constantly, until the sauce boils and thickens. Reduce the heat and simmer for 2 minutes more before stirring in the parsley and a little salt and pepper. Serve over the slices of beef with steamed vegetables.

Serves 6

Dessert

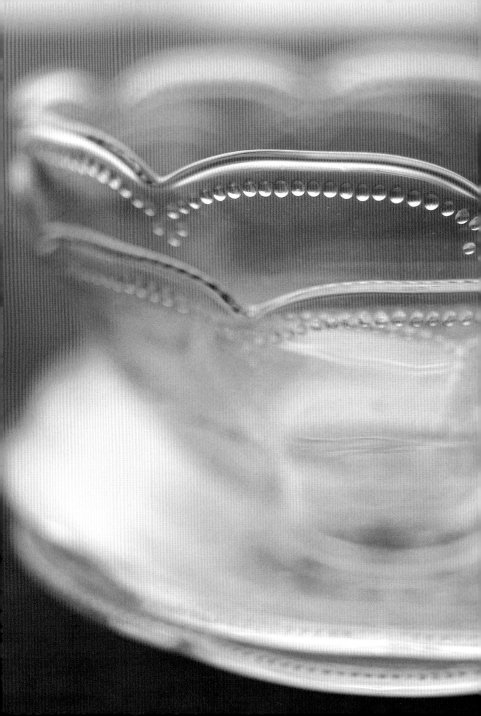

Double chocolate brownies

5$\frac{1}{2}$ tablespoons butter
$\frac{1}{3}$ cup cocoa powder
$\frac{2}{3}$ cup superfine sugar
2 eggs
$\frac{1}{2}$ cup all-purpose flour
$\frac{1}{2}$ teaspoon baking powder
$\frac{1}{2}$ cup chocolate chips

Preheat the oven on to 350°F. Brush an 8-inch square pan with oil or melted butter and put a piece of baking parchment on the bottom.

Melt the butter in a saucepan. When it is ready, take it off the heat and stir in the cocoa and sugar, followed by the eggs.

Put a sieve over the saucepan and add the flour and baking powder, along with a pinch of salt. Sift everything into the saucepan, then mix it in. Make sure you don't have any pockets of flour. Add the chocolate chips and stir them in.

Pour the mixture into the pan and bake it for 30 minutes. If you have used a different-sized pan, the cooking time may be shorter (bigger pan) or longer (smaller pan). You will know your brownies are cooked when you can poke a knife into the middle and it comes out clean. Remember, though, the chocolate chips may have melted and if your knife hits one of them, it might look as if the mixture is still wet. Leave the brownies to cool in the pan, then cut into squares.

Makes 12

Tropical meringues

3 egg whites
3/4 cup superfine sugar
1/2 cup dried coconut
1/4 teaspoon coconut extract
2 tablespoons milk
2 tablespoons superfine sugar, extra
9 oz. mascarpone cheese
2 mangoes, peeled and thinly sliced
2 passion fruit

Preheat the oven to 275°F. Grease and line two baking sheets with baking parchment. Put the egg whites in a bowl and whisk until soft peaks form. Add the sugar, a tablespoon at a time, until the mixture is glossy. Fold in the dried coconut and coconut extract.

Spoon 3-in. mounds of the mixture onto the sheets. Bake for 1 hour. Turn the oven off and leave the meringues in the oven for another hour.

Add the milk and sugar to the mascarpone and whisk well. Dollop a little onto each meringue and top with the passion fruit.

Makes 6

Chocolate-chip and pistachio friands

1³/₄ cups shelled pistachio nuts
¹/₂ cup all-purpose flour
³/₄ cup unsalted butter
1²/₃ cups confectioners' sugar
2 tablespoons cocoa
¹/₂ teaspoon ground cardamom
5 egg whites, lightly whisked
1 cup chocolate chips
confectioners' sugar, extra, to dust

Preheat the oven to 400°F. Grease and line ten friand tins or ten ¹/₂-cup muffin tins. Place the pistachios on a baking tray and roast for 5 minutes. Remove from the oven and allow to cool. Place the pistachios and flour in a food processor and process until finely ground.

Place the butter and confectioners' sugar in a bowl and beat until light and creamy. Sift together the pistachios and flour with the cocoa and cardamom and fold into the creamed mixture.

Stir the egg whites into the creamed mixture, together with the chocolate chips, and mix to combine. Spoon the mixture into the prepared tins and bake for 25–30 minutes or until they come away from the sides of the tins. Cool on wire racks. Dust lightly with icing sugar.

Makes 10

Chocolate-hazelnut puff pastry rolls

5$^1/_2$ tablespoons chocolate-hazelnut spread
$^2/_3$ cup confectioners' sugar
2 sheets puff pastry, thawed
1 egg, lightly beaten
confectioners' sugar, extra, to dust

Preheat the oven to 400°F. Combine the chocolate-hazelnut spread and confectioners' sugar and roll into an 8-in.-long roll. Wrap the roll in plastic wrap and twist the ends to enclose. Refrigerate for 30 minutes. When firm, cut the roll into eight even pieces. Roll each of the pieces in confectioners' sugar.

Cut each sheet of puff pastry into four squares. Place a piece of the chocolate-hazelnut mixture roll onto each square of pastry and roll up to enclose. Pinch the ends and brush lightly with egg. Bake for 15 minutes or until the pastry is golden.

Dust with confectioners' sugar.

Serves 4

High-top cappuccino and white-chocolate muffins

1/4 cup instant espresso coffee
  powder
1 tablespoon boiling water
2 1/2 cups self-rising flour
1/2 cup superfine sugar
2 eggs, lightly beaten
1 1/2 cups buttermilk
1 teaspoon vanilla extract
3/4 cup butter, melted
3 1/2 oz. white chocolate, roughly
  chopped
2 tablespoons butter, extra
3 tablespoons brown sugar

Preheat the oven to 400°F. Cut eight lengths of baking parchment and roll into 3-in.-high cylinders to fit into eight 1/2-cup ramekins. When in place in the ramekins, secure the cylinders with string and place all the ramekins on a baking sheet.

Dissolve the coffee in the boiling water and allow to cool. Sift the flour and sugar into a bowl. Combine the egg, buttermilk, vanilla, melted butter, white chocolate, and the coffee mixture and roughly combine with the dry ingredients. Spoon the mixture into each cylinder.

Heat the extra butter and the brown sugar and stir until the sugar dissolves. Spoon this mixture onto each muffin and gently swirl into the muffin using a skewer. Bake for 25–30 minutes or until risen and cooked when tested with a skewer.

Makes 8

Nursery rice pudding

²/₃ cup arborio or short-grain rice
4 cups milk
¹/₃ cup superfine sugar
1 teaspoon vanilla extract
¹/₂ cup cream

Rinse the rice in a colander until the water runs clear. Drain well and place in a heavy-bottomed pan with the milk, sugar, and vanilla.

Bring to a boil while stirring, then reduce the heat to the lowest setting and cook for about 45 minutes, stirring frequently, until the rice is thick and creamy.

Remove the pan from the heat and let stand for 10 minutes. Stir in the cream. Serve warm with stewed fruit, if desired.

Serves 4–6

Variations: Add a cinnamon stick and a strip of lemon zest to the rice in place of vanilla extract. Or add a small sprig of washed lavender to the rice while cooking.

Zabaglione

6 egg yolks
3 tablespoons superfine sugar
$\frac{1}{2}$ cup sweet Marsala
1 cup heavy cream

Whisk the egg yolks and sugar in the top of a double boiler or in a heatproof bowl set over a saucepan of simmering water. Make sure that the base of the bowl does not touch the water or the egg may overcook and stick. It is important that you whisk constantly to move the cooked mixture from the outside of the bowl to the center.

When the mixture is tepid, add the Marsala and whisk for another 5 minutes or until it has thickened enough to hold its shape when drizzled off the whisk into the bowl.

Whip the cream until soft peaks form. Gently fold in the egg yolk and Marsala mixture. Divide among four glasses or bowls. Cover and refrigerate for 3–4 hours before serving.

Serves 4

Grandmother's pavlova

4 egg whites
1 cup superfine sugar
2 teaspoons cornstarch
1 teaspoon white vinegar
2 cups cream
3 passion fruit, to decorate
strawberries, halved, to decorate

Preheat the oven to 315°F. Line a baking tray with baking parchment.

Place the egg whites and a pinch of salt in a small, dry bowl. Using electric beaters, beat until stiff peaks form. Add the sugar gradually, beating constantly after each addition, until the mixture is thick and glossy and all the sugar has dissolved.

Using a metal spoon, fold in the cornstarch and vinegar. Spoon the mixture into a mound on the prepared tray. Lightly flatten the top of the pavlova and smooth the sides. (This pavlova should have a cake shape and be about 1 in. high.) Bake for 1 hour or until pale cream and crisp. Remove from the oven while warm and carefully turn upside down onto a plate. Allow to cool.

Lightly whip the cream until soft peaks form and spread over the soft center. Decorate with pulp from the passion fruit and halved strawberries. Cut into wedges to serve.

Serves 6

Trifle

4 slices of pound cake or sponge
  cake
3 tablespoons sweet sherry or
  Madeira
1 cup raspberries
4 eggs
2 tablespoons superfine sugar
2 tablespoons all-purpose flour
2 cups milk
1/4 teaspoon vanilla extract
1/2 cup cream, whipped
3 tablespoons flaked almonds,
  to decorate
raspberries, extra, to decorate

Put the cake in the base of a bowl, then sprinkle it with the sherry. Sprinkle the raspberries over the top and crush them gently into the cake with the back of a spoon to release their tart flavor, leaving some of them whole.

Mix the eggs, sugar, and flour together in a bowl. Heat the milk in a pan, pour it over the egg mixture, stir well, and pour back into a clean pan. Cook over medium heat until the custard boils and thickens and coats the back of a spoon. Stir in the vanilla, cover the surface with plastic wrap, and leave to cool.

Pour the cooled custard over the raspberries and leave to set in the refrigerator—it will firm up but not become solid. Spoon the whipped cream over the custard. Go wild decorating with almonds and raspberries (or anything else you like) and refrigerate until ready to serve.

Serves 6

Creamy chocolate mousse

4½ oz. good-quality dark chocolate,
  chopped
4 eggs, separated
¾ cup cream, lightly whipped
cocoa powder, to serve

Melt the chocolate in a bowl over a saucepan of gently simmering water (make sure the base of the bowl does not touch the water). Stir the chocolate occasionally until it's melted, then take it off the heat to cool slightly. Lightly beat the egg yolks and stir them into the melted chocolate, then gently fold in the cream until velvety.

Beat the egg whites to soft peaks. Fold one spoonful of the fluffy egg white into the mousse with a metal spoon, then gently fold in the remainder—the secret is to use a light, quick touch.

You only need small quantities of the mousse—you can either serve it in six small wine glasses or ¾-cup ramekins. Cover with plastic wrap and refrigerate for 4 hours or overnight until set. When you're ready to serve, add a curl of whipped cream and a dusting of cocoa powder.

Serves 6

Banana fritters

1 cup self-rising flour
1 tablespoon superfine sugar
1 teaspoon ground cinnamon
4 bananas
vegetable oil, for deep-frying
ice cream, to serve

Sift the flour and a pinch of salt into a bowl. Make a well in the center, then gradually add 1 cup water while gently whisking, drawing the flour in from the sides. Whisk until just combined. Don't worry if the batter looks a bit lumpy. Let stand for 30 minutes. Combine the sugar and cinnamon in a bowl, and set aside.

Cut the bananas in half crosswise, slightly on the diagonal. Dip them into the batter. Quickly drain off any excess batter and deep-fry for 2 minutes or until crisp and golden. The best way to do this is to use two pairs of tongs—one to dip the bananas in the batter and lift into the oil, and one to remove from the oil. You could also use a slotted spoon to lift the cooked fritters. Drain on paper towels. Repeat with the remaining bananas. Sprinkle with the cinnamon sugar and serve with ice cream.

Serves 4

Baked cheesecake

13 oz. vanilla wafers
$^3/_4$ cup unsalted butter, melted

Filling
2$^1/_4$ cups cream cheese
scant 1 cup superfine sugar
4 eggs
1$^1/_4$ cups whipping cream
2 tablespoons all-purpose flour
1 teaspoon ground cinnamon
$^1/_4$ teaspoon freshly grated nutmeg
1 tablespoon lemon juice
2 teaspoons vanilla extract
freshly grated nutmeg, extra
ground cinnamon
cream, to serve
strawberries, to serve

Process the wafers in a food processor until they are crushed into fine crumbs. Add the melted butter and process for another 10 seconds. Press the mixture into the base and sides of a lightly greased, shallow, 9-in. springform pan, then place it in the refrigerator for an hour.

Beat the cream cheese and sugar together, then add the eggs and cream and beat for about 4 minutes. Fold in the flour, cinnamon, nutmeg, lemon juice, and vanilla. Pour the mixture into the chilled crust. Bake in a 350°F oven for an hour without opening the oven door, until the cheesecake is golden brown on top.

Turn off the heat and let the cake stand in the oven for 2 hours. Open the oven door and let it stand for another hour. Refrigerate overnight.

For a decorative touch, sprinkle with nutmeg and cinnamon and then serve. Delicious with lashings of cream and some strawberries.

Serves 10

Chocolate croissant bake

4 croissants, torn into pieces
4½ oz. good-quality dark chocolate,
  chopped into pieces
4 eggs
5 tablespoons superfine sugar
1 cup milk
1 cup cream
1 tablespoon orange liqueur
1 tablespoon grated orange zest
4 tablespoons orange juice
2 tablespoons roughly chopped
  hazelnuts
cream, to serve

Preheat the oven to 350°F. Grease the base and side of a deep-sided, 8-in. cake pan and line the bottom of the pan with baking parchment. Put the croissant pieces into the pan, then sprinkle with three-quarters of the chopped chocolate pieces.

Beat the eggs and sugar together until pale and creamy. Heat the milk, cream, liqueur, and remaining chocolate pieces in a saucepan until almost boiling. Stir to melt the chocolate, then remove the pan from the heat. Gradually add to the egg mixture, stirring constantly. Next, stir in the orange zest and juice. Slowly pour the mixture over the croissants, allowing the liquid to be fully absorbed before adding more.

Sprinkle the hazelnuts over the top and bake for 50 minutes or until a skewer comes out clean when inserted into the center. Cool for 10 minutes. Turn out and invert onto a serving plate. Slice and serve warm with a dollop of cream.

Serves 6–8

Baked rice pudding

¼ cup short- or medium-grain rice
1⅔ cups milk
1½ tablespoons superfine sugar
¾ cup cream
¼ teaspoon vanilla extract
¼ teaspoon grated nutmeg
1 bay leaf (optional)

Preheat the oven to 300°F and grease four 1-cup ramekins. In a bowl, mix together the rice, milk, sugar, cream, and vanilla extract and pour into the greased dish. Dust the surface with the grated nutmeg and float the bay leaf on top for a little extra flavor.

Bake the rice puddings for about 1 hour, until the rice has absorbed most of the milk, the texture is creamy, and a brown skin has formed on top. Serve hot.

Serves 4

Eton mess

4–6 ready-made meringues
1 cup strawberries
1 teaspoon superfine sugar
1 cup heavy cream

Break the meringues into pieces. Cut the strawberries into quarters and put them in a bowl with the sugar. Using a potato masher or the back of a spoon, squash them slightly so they start to become juicy. Whip the cream with a whisk or electric beater until it is quite thick but not solid.

Mix everything together gently and spoon it into glasses, then serve.

Serves 4

Lemon pudding with citrus cream

4½ tablespoons butter, softened
¾ cup sugar
2 teaspoons grated lemon zest
3 eggs, separated
¼ cup self-rising flour
¾ cup milk
⅓ cup lemon juice

Citrus cream
1¼ cups heavy cream
2 tablespoons confectioners' sugar
grated zest of 1 orange
grated zest of ½ lime
confectioners' sugar, extra, to serve

Preheat the oven to 350°F. Lightly grease a 4-cup round ovenproof or soufflé dish. Put the butter, sugar, and lemon zest in a bowl and beat until light and well combined.

Add the egg yolks gradually, beating well after each addition. Add the flour and milk alternately to make a smooth but not runny batter. Stir in the lemon juice. The batter may seem to have separated at this stage, but this is fine.

In a separate bowl, whisk the egg whites until firm (but not dry) peaks form, then use a metal spoon to gently fold the whites into the batter. Pour the batter into the ovenproof dish and place into a roasting pan. Fill the pan with enough boiling water to come one-third of the way up the outside of the dish. Cook for 40–45 minutes or until risen and firm to the touch. Allow to stand for 10 minutes before serving.

Meanwhile, make the citrus cream. Whip the cream with the sugar until soft peaks form. Fold in the grated orange and lime zest. Dust the pudding with confectioners' sugar, if you like, and serve with the citrus cream.

Serves 4–6

Individual sticky date cakes

1½ cups pitted dates, chopped
1 teaspoon baking soda
¾ cup unsalted butter, chopped
1½ cups self-rising flour
1⅓ cups brown sugar
2 eggs, lightly beaten
2 tablespoons dark corn syrup
¾ cup cream

Preheat the oven to 350°F. Grease six 1-cup muffin tins. Put the dates and 1 cup water in a saucepan, bring to a boil, then remove from the heat and stir in the baking soda. Add ¼ cup of the butter and stir until melted.

Sift the flour into a large bowl, then stir in ½ cup of the sugar. Make a well in the center, add the date mixture and eggs, and stir until combined. Evenly divide the mixture among the muffin tins and bake for 20 minutes or until a skewer comes out clean when inserted into the center.

To make the sauce, put the corn syrup, cream, and the remaining butter and sugar in a small saucepan and stir over low heat for 4 minutes or until the sugar has dissolved. Bring to a boil, then reduce the heat and simmer, stirring occasionally, for 2 minutes.

To serve, put the warm cakes onto serving plates, pierce a few times with a skewer, and drizzle with the sauce. Serve with ice cream, if desired.

Makes 6

Spiced fruit salad

½ cup superfine sugar
4 slices ginger
1 bird's-eye chili, cut in half
juice and zest of 2 limes
a mixture of watermelon, melon,
  mangoes, bananas, cherries,
  lychees, kiwi fruit, or anything else
  you like—enough for 4 servings
ice cream, to serve

Put the sugar in a saucepan with
½ cup water and the ginger and chili.
Heat it until the sugar melts, then let
cool before adding the lime juice and
zest. Take out the ginger and chili.

Put your selection of fruit into a bowl
and pour the syrup over it. Leave it to
marinate in the fridge for 30 minutes.
Serve with coconut ice cream or any
other kind of ice cream or sorbet.

Serves 4

Crème caramel

Caramel
½ cup superfine sugar

2¾ cups milk
1 vanilla bean
½ cup superfine sugar
3 eggs, beaten
3 egg yolks

To make the caramel, put the sugar in a heavy-bottomed saucepan and heat until it dissolves and starts to caramelize—tip the saucepan from side to side as the sugar cooks to keep the coloring even. Remove from the heat and carefully add 2 tablespoons water to stop the cooking process. Pour into six ½-cup ramekins and leave to cool.

Preheat the oven to 350°F. Put the milk and vanilla pod in a saucepan and bring just to a boil. Mix together the sugar, egg, and egg yolks. Strain the boiling milk over the egg mixture and stir well. Ladle into the ramekins and place in a roasting pan. Pour enough hot water into the pan to come halfway up the sides of the ramekins. Cook for 35–40 minutes or until firm to the touch. Remove from the pan and leave for 15 minutes. Unmold onto plates and top with any leftover caramel.

Serves 6

Zuppa inglese

4 thick slices sponge cake
$\frac{1}{3}$ cup kirsch
$\frac{1}{2}$ cup raspberries
$\frac{1}{2}$ cup blackberries
2 tablespoons superfine sugar
1 cup custard
1 cup cream, lightly whipped
confectioners' sugar, to dust

Put a piece of sponge cake on each of four deep plates and brush or sprinkle it with the kirsch. Leave the kirsch to soak in for at least a minute or two.

Put the raspberries and blackberries in a saucepan with the sugar. Gently warm through over low heat so that the sugar just melts, then leave the fruit to cool.

Spoon the fruit over the sponge cake, pour the custard on top of the fruit, and, finally, dollop the cream on top and dust with confectioners' sugar.

Serves 4

Baked apples

6 cooking apples
5 tablespoons unsalted butter, chilled
6 small cinnamon sticks
$3/4$ cup pistachio nuts or pine nuts
3 tablespoons brown sugar
$1/2$ cup raisins or golden raisins
scant 1 cup grappa

Preheat the oven to 350°F. Remove the cores from the apples with a sharp knife or corer and place the apples in an ovenproof dish.

Divide the butter into six cubes and push a cube into the core of each apple. Push a cinnamon stick into the middle of each apple and sprinkle with the nuts, sugar, and raisins. Finally, pour the grappa over the apples.

Bake for 30–35 minutes, basting the apples occasionally with the juices in the dish, until they are soft when tested with a skewer.

Serves 4

Mango fool

2 very ripe mangoes
1 cup plain yogurt
⅓ cup cream

Take the flesh off the mangoes. The easiest way to do this is to slice down either side of the pit so you have two "cheeks." Make crisscross cuts through the mango flesh on each cheek, almost through to the skin, then turn each cheek inside out and slice the flesh from the skin into a bowl. Cut the rest of the flesh from the pits.

Puree the flesh either by using a food processor or blender.

Put a spoonful of mango puree in the bottom of four small glasses, bowls, or cups, put a spoonful of yogurt on top, and then repeat. Spoon a little cream over each serving when you have used up all the mango and yogurt. Swirl the layers together just before eating.

Serves 4

Tiramisu

5 eggs, separated
$3/4$ cup superfine sugar
9 oz. mascarpone cheese
1 cup cold very strong coffee
3 tablespoons brandy or sweet
  Marsala
44 small ladyfinger cookies
$2^3/4$ oz. dark chocolate, finely grated

Beat the egg yolks with the sugar until the sugar has dissolved and the mixture is light and fluffy and leaves a ribbon trail when dropped from the whisk. Add the mascarpone and beat until the mixture is smooth. Whisk the egg whites in a clean, dry glass bowl until soft peaks form. Fold into the mascarpone mixture.

Pour the coffee into a shallow dish and add the brandy. Dip some of the ladyfingers into the coffee mixture, using enough to cover the base of a 10-in. square dish. The ladyfingers should be fairly well soaked on both sides but not so much so that they break up. Arrange the ladyfingers in one tightly packed layer in the base of the dish.

Spread half the mascarpone mixture over the ladyfingers. Add another layer of soaked ladyfingers and then another layer of mascarpone, smoothing the top layer neatly. Refrigerate for at least 2 hours or overnight. Dust with the grated chocolate before serving.

Serves 4

White chocolate creams

1 cup heavy cream
4 cardamom pods, slightly crushed
1 bay leaf
5½ oz. white chocolate
3 egg yolks

Put the cream, cardamom, and bay leaf in a saucepan and gently bring the mixture to a boil. Remove from the heat and set aside so the cardamom and bay leaf flavors infuse into the cream.

Grate or finely chop the white chocolate—this will make it melt much faster and also lessen the chance of it becoming lumpy—and put it in a bowl. Gently heat the cream up again until it is almost boiling and then pour it through a sieve (to strain out the cardamom and bay leaf) over the chocolate. Stir until the chocolate has dissolved. Gently whisk the egg yolks and stir them into the mixture.

Pour the mixture into four espresso cups or really small bowls and refrigerate for a couple of hours to set.

Serves 4

Panna cotta

2 cups heavy cream
4 tablespoons superfine sugar
2 tablespoons grappa (optional)
vanilla extract
1 1/4 teaspoons powdered gelatin
1 cup berries, to serve

Put the cream and sugar in a saucepan and stir over gentle heat until the sugar has dissolved. Bring to a boil, then simmer for 3 minutes, adding the grappa and a few drops of vanilla extract to taste.

Sprinkle the powdered gelatin onto the hot cream in an even layer and leave it to absorb for a minute, then stir it into the cream until dissolved.

Pour the mixture into four 1/2-cup metal or ceramic ramekins, cover each with a piece of plastic wrap, and refrigerate until set.

Unmold the panna cotta by placing the ramekins very briefly in a bowl of hot water and then tipping them gently onto plates. Metal ramekins will take a shorter time than ceramic to unmold, as they heat up quickly. Serve with fresh berries.

Serves 4

Fig and raspberry cake

3/4 cup unsalted butter
3/4 cup superfine sugar, plus extra for
   sprinkling
1 egg, plus 1 egg yolk
2²/₃ cups all-purpose flour
1 teaspoon baking powder
4 figs, quartered
grated zest of 1 orange
1 cup raspberries

Preheat the oven to 350°F. Lightly grease a 9-in. springform pan. Cream the butter and sugar until light. Add the egg and yolk and beat again. Sift in the flour, baking powder, and a pinch of salt and combine to form a dough. Chill until firm.

Divide the dough in two and roll one piece out large enough to cover the bottom of the pan. Transfer it to the prepared pan and set in place, pressing the dough up the sides a little. Cover with the figs, orange zest, and raspberries. Roll out the remaining dough and place it over the filling. Brush with water and sprinkle with a little sugar. Bake for 30 minutes and serve warm.

Serves 6

Chocolate dessert

6 oz. dark chocolate, chopped
butter, for greasing
1/3 cup superfine sugar
2 1/4 oz. milk chocolate, chopped
4 eggs
cream, to serve

Preheat the oven to 400°F. Put the dark chocolate in a glass bowl and set it above a pan of simmering water. The chocolate will gradually start to soften and look glossy—when it does this, stir it until it is smooth.

Grease the inside of four 1-cup ramekins or ovenproof bowls with butter. Add 1/2 teaspoon of the sugar to each and shake it around until the insides are coated. Divide the chopped milk chocolate among the ramekins.

Beat the rest of the sugar with the egg yolks, using electric beaters, for about 3 minutes or until you have a pale, creamy mass. Clean the beaters and dry them thoroughly. Whisk the egg whites until they are thick enough to stand up in peaks.

Fold the melted chocolate into the yolk mixture and then fold in the whites. Use a large spoon or rubber spatula to do this and try not to squash out too much air. Divide the mixture among the ramekins. Bake for 15–20 minutes. The desserts should be puffed and spongelike. Serve immediately with cream.

Serves 4

Sticky black rice pudding with mangoes

2 cups black sticky rice
3 fresh pandanus leaves (1 teaspoon
  vanilla may be substituted)
2 cups coconut milk
1/2 cup brown sugar
3 tablespoons superfine sugar
coconut cream, to serve
mango or papaya cubes, to serve

Put the rice in a large glass or ceramic bowl and cover with water. Leave to soak for at least 8 hours or overnight. Drain, then put in a saucepan with 4 cups of water and slowly bring to a boil. Cook at a simmer, stirring frequently, for 20 minutes or until tender. Drain.

Shred the pandanus leaves with your fingers, then tie them in a knot. Pour the coconut milk into a large saucepan and heat until almost boiling. Add the brown sugar, superfine sugar, and pandanus leaves and stir until the sugar is dissolved.

Add the rice to the pan and cook, stirring, for about 8 minutes without boiling. Remove from the heat, cover, and leave for 15 minutes to absorb the flavors. Remove the pandanus leaves.

Spoon the rice into individual bowls and serve warm with coconut cream and fresh mango or papaya cubes.

Serves 6

Coffee gelato

5 egg yolks
$\frac{1}{2}$ cup sugar
2 cups milk
$\frac{1}{2}$ cup freshly made espresso
1 tablespoon Tia Maria or coffee
  liqueur

Whisk the egg yolks and half the sugar in a bowl until you have a pale and creamy mixture. Pour the milk and coffee into a saucepan, add the remaining sugar, and bring to a boil. Add to the egg mixture and whisk together. Pour back into the saucepan and cook over low heat, being careful that the custard doesn't boil. Stir constantly until the mixture is thick enough to coat the back of a wooden spoon. Strain the custard into a bowl and cool over ice before adding the Tia Maria.

To make the gelato by hand, pour the mixture into a bowl, cover, and freeze. Break up the ice crystals every 30 minutes with a fork to ensure a smooth texture. Repeat until it is ready—this may take 4 hours. If using an ice-cream machine, follow the manufacturer's instructions.

Serves 6

Apple crumble

8 apples
$\frac{1}{3}$ cup superfine sugar
zest of 1 lemon
$\frac{1}{2}$ cup butter
1 cup all-purpose flour
1 teaspoon ground cinnamon
cream, to serve

Preheat the oven to 350°. Peel and core the apples, then cut them into chunks. Put the apples, 2 tablespoons of the sugar, and the lemon zest in a small baking dish and mix them together. Dot with 2 tablespoons of butter.

Rub the remaining butter into the flour until you have a texture that resembles coarse bread crumbs. Stir in the rest of the sugar and the cinnamon. Add 1–2 tablespoons of water and stir the crumbs together so they form bigger clumps.

Sprinkle the crumble mixture over the apples and bake the crumble for 1 hour 15 minutes, by which time the top should be browned and the juice bubbling up through the crumble. Serve with cream.

Serves 4

Fruit poached in red wine

3 pears, peeled, quartered, and cored
3 apples, peeled, quartered, and
   cored
3 tablespoons sugar
1 vanilla pod, cut in half lengthwise
2 small cinnamon sticks
$1^3/_4$ cups red wine
scant 1 cup dessert wine or port
1 lb. 9 oz. red-skinned plums, halved
ice cream, to serve
cookies, to serve

Put the pears and apples in a large saucepan. Add the sugar, vanilla pod, cinnamon sticks, red wine, and dessert wine and bring to a boil. Reduce the heat and gently simmer for about 5–10 minutes or until just soft.

Add the plums, stirring them into the pears and apples, and bring the liquid back to a simmer. Cook for another 5 minutes or until the plums are soft.

Remove the saucepan from the heat, cover with a lid, and leave the fruit to marinate in the syrup for at least 6 hours. Reheat gently to serve warm or serve at room temperature with cream or ice cream and cookies.

Serves 6

Coffee granita

scant 1 cup superfine sugar
5 cups very strong espresso coffee
ice cream, to serve

Heat the sugar with 1 tablespoon hot water in a saucepan until the sugar dissolves. Simmer for 3 minutes to make a sugar syrup. Add the coffee and stir well.

Pour into a shallow plastic or metal dish. The mixture should be no deeper than 1 1/4 in. so that the granita freezes quickly and breaks up easily. Stir every 2 hours with a fork to break up the ice crystals as they form. Repeat this two or three times. The granita is ready when almost set but still grainy. Stir a fork through it just before serving. Serve with ice cream.

Serves 6

Chocolate and almond torte

1 cup sliced or whole almonds
1 slice panettone or 1 small brioche
10½ oz. dark chocolate
2 tablespoons brandy
²/₃ cup unsalted butter, softened
²/₃ cup superfine sugar
4 eggs
1 teaspoon vanilla extract (optional)
7 oz. mascarpone cheese
cocoa powder, to dust
crème fraîche, to serve

Preheat the oven to 325°F. Toast the almonds in the oven for 8–10 minutes until golden brown.

Put the almonds and panettone in a food processor and process until the mixture resembles bread crumbs. Grease a 9-in. springform pan with a little butter. Put some of the mixture into the pan and shake it around so that it forms a coating on the bottom and side of the pan. Put the remaining nut mixture aside.

Gently melt the chocolate and brandy in a heatproof bowl set over a saucepan of simmering water, making sure that the bowl does not touch the water. Stir occasionally until the chocolate has melted. Cool slightly.

Cream the butter and sugar in the food processor or with a wooden spoon for a few minutes until light and pale. Add the melted chocolate, eggs, vanilla, and mascarpone. Add the remaining nut mixture and mix well. Pour into the pan.

Bake for 50–60 minutes or until just set. Leave to rest in the pan for about 15 minutes before taking out. Dust with a little cocoa when cool and serve with crème fraîche.

Venetian rice pudding

3 cups milk
1 cup heavy cream
1 vanilla pod, split
¼ cup superfine sugar
¼ teaspoon ground cinnamon
pinch of grated nutmeg
1 tablespoon grated orange zest
½ cup raisins
2 tablespoons brandy or sweet
  Marsala
½ cup arborio or short-grain rice

Put the milk, cream, and vanilla pod in a heavy-bottomed saucepan and bring just to a boil, then remove from the heat. Add the sugar, cinnamon, nutmeg, and orange zest and set aside.

Put the raisins and brandy in a small bowl and leave to soak. Add the rice to the infused milk and return to the heat. Bring to a simmer and stir slowly for 35 minutes or until the rice is creamy. Stir in the raisins and remove the vanilla pod at the end of cooking. Serve warm or cold.

Serves 4

Chocolate affogato

9 oz. dark chocolate
4 cups milk
6 eggs
½ cup superfine sugar
1⅓ cups heavy cream
4 small cups of espresso or very
   strong coffee
4 shots Frangelico or any other
   liqueur

Break the chocolate into individual squares and put it with the milk in a saucepan. Heat the milk over low heat—you must do this slowly or the chocolate will stick to the bottom. As the milk heats up and the chocolate melts, stir the mixture until you have a smooth liquid. You don't need to boil the milk, as the chocolate will melt at a much lower temperature.

Whisk the eggs and sugar together with electric beaters in a large glass or metal bowl until the mixture is pale and frothy. Add the milk and chocolate mixture, along with the cream, and mix.

Pour the mixture into a shallow plastic or metal container and put it in the freezer. In order to make a smooth ice cream you will now have to whisk the mixture every hour or so to break up the ice crystals as they form. When the mixture gets very stiff, let it set overnight.

Scoop four balls of ice cream out of the container and put them into four cups, then put these in the freezer while you make the coffee.

Serve the ice cream with the Frangelico and coffee poured over it.

Serves 4

Basics

Boiling rice

Rinse the rice under cold running water until the water running away is clear, then drain well.

Put the rice in a heavy-bottomed saucepan and add enough water to come about 2 in. above the surface of the rice. Add 1 teaspoon of salt and bring the water quickly to a boil. When it boils, cover and reduce the heat to a simmer.

Cook for 15 minutes, or until the rice is just tender, then remove the saucepan from the heat and let stand for 10 minutes without removing the lid. Fluff the rice with a fork before serving.

Cooking noodles

Some noodles need to be softened in boiling water; others are cooked or fried, so always refer to the instructions on the package. Cook noodles in plenty of boiling water and drain well.

If cooking small or individual portions of fresh noodles, put them in a sieve and dunk them in a saucepan of boiling water. This is a good method for quick-cooking noodles, such as egg or rice noodles.

Cold noodles can be tossed in a little oil to keep them from sticking, then reheated in boiling water.

Cooking pasta

Pasta has to be cooked in lots of rapidly boiling salted water—about 4 cups of water and 1 teaspoon salt per 3 1/2 oz. of pasta. The pan must be large enough for the pasta to move about freely.

It is not necessary to add oil to the cooking water or the draining pasta; all this does is coat the pasta and encourage the sauce to slide off.

When you drain pasta, don't do it too thoroughly—a little water left clinging to the pasta will help the sauce spread through it.

Pizza dough

Mix 2 teaspoons dried yeast with 1 tablespoon sugar and 1/3 cup warm water and leave until the mixture bubbles.

Sift 4 cups all-purpose flour into a bowl with a pinch of salt, add the yeast and 1/2 cup water, and mix to a soft dough.

Knead the dough until smooth and springy—at least 5 minutes. Put in a bowl, cover, and leave to rise until doubled in size.

Punch the air out of the dough with your fist and divide it into two equal pieces.

Flatten each piece of dough into a circle, then, working from the center out, make the circle bigger using the heel of your hand.

Leave a slightly raised rim around the edge and place it on an oiled baking sheet dusted with cornmeal. Add the toppings.

Mashed potatoes

Peel and chop 4 large russet potatoes. Put them in cold water and bring them to a boil. Boil until tender, drain well, and put them back in a saucepan over a low heat with 2 tablespoons of hot milk, 1 tablespoon of butter, and plenty of salt and pepper.

Remove from the stove and mash with a masher, then beat with a wooden spoon until fluffy. You can add more butter, a grating of nutmeg, or a splash of cream. Serves 4.

Risotto

Use a large, deep frying pan or shallow saucepan with a heavy base. Make sure the stock or liquid you are going to add is hot—keep it at a low simmer on the stove.

Cook the rice in the butter first. This creates a seal around the grains, trapping the starch. Stir frequently to prevent the rice from sticking to the bottom of the pan and to ensure all the grains are cooked evenly.

Add the liquid a ladleful at a time. Stir constantly. If you cook the rice too slowly it will become gluey; too fast and the liquid will evaporate—keep it at a fast simmer.

Season the rice early, while it is absorbing flavors. Add just enough liquid to cover it so it cooks evenly. The rice should be al dente. Stop cooking the rice as soon as it is creamy but still has a little texture in the middle of the grain. The risotto should be rich and thick like oatmeal, not too wet or dry.

Chicken stock

Put 4$\frac{1}{2}$ lb. chicken bones, trimmings, wings, and necks in a large saucepan with 2 chopped carrots, 1 halved onion, 1 chopped leek, 1 chopped celery stalk, a bouquet garni, and 6 peppercorns. Add 16 cups of cold water.

Bring to a boil and skim off any froth. Simmer the stock for 2 hours, skimming at regular intervals (adding a splash of cold water will bring up any scum).

Strain the stock and let cool in the refrigerator. When it's cold, you can lift off the layer of fat from the top.

Vegetable stock

Put 1 lb. 2 oz. mixed chopped carrots, celery, onions, and leeks in a saucepan with a bouquet garni and 10 peppercorns.

Add 10 cups cold water and bring to the boil. Skim off any scum.

Simmer the stock for 1–2 hours, pressing the solids to extract all the flavor, then strain and cool in the refrigerator.

Fish stock

Put 4 lb. 8 oz. fish bones and heads, a bouquet garni, 1 chopped onion, and 10 peppercorns in the pot.

Add 10 cups cold water and bring to a boil and simmer for 20–30 minutes. Skim off any scum.

Strain the stock, then cool in the refrigerator. When cool, lift off any congealed fat.

Pesto

Put 2 garlic cloves in a mortar and pestle or food processor and add a pinch of salt and 1/4 cup pine nuts. Pound or whizz to a paste.

Gradually add 1 cup basil leaves and pound or whizz the leaves into the base mixture. Stir in 1/2 cup grated Parmesan cheese, then gradually add 1/2 cup olive oil.

Use immediately or store covered in the refrigerator for up to 1 week. If storing, make sure the pesto surface is covered with a thin layer of olive oil. Makes 1 cup.

Vinaigrette

Using a mortar and pestle, or the blade of a knife, crush 1 small garlic clove with a little salt to form a smooth paste. Add 1 tablespoon of good-quality vinegar and 1/2 teaspoon of Dijon mustard and mix well.

Gradually mix in 3 tablespoons of olive oil until a smooth emulsion is formed. Season with salt and pepper. Makes enough for one salad.

Melting chocolate

When melting chocolate, always use a clean, dry bowl. Water or moisture will make the chocolate seize (turn into a thick mass that won't melt), and overheating will make it scorch and taste bitter.

To melt chocolate, chop it into small, even-sized pieces and place in a heatproof bowl. Bring a saucepan of water to a boil, then remove from the heat. Sit the bowl over the saucepan of water—make sure the bowl doesn't touch the water and that no water or steam gets into the bowl or the chocolate will seize. Leave the chocolate to soften a little, then stir until smooth and melted.

Remove the chocolate from the saucepan to cool, or leave in place over the hot water if you want to keep the chocolate liquid.

Meringue

To make meringue, beat 6 egg whites and a pinch of cream of tartar in a clean, dry bowl with electric beaters until soft peaks form. Gradually pour in 1$\frac{1}{2}$ cups superfine sugar, beating until the meringue is thick and glossy.

Whipping cream

Before whipping cream, chill the mixing bowl in the refrigerator.

For maximum volume, use a balloon whisk and beat well. You can use an electric beater, but make sure you don't overbeat the cream and end up with butter.

Beating egg whites

Eggs for whisking should be at room temperature as cold egg whites will not whisk well. Always use a very clean and dry glass or metal bowl. Whisk the whites gently at first, then more vigorously until you reach the stage you want, ensuring you have beaten all the egg to the same degree.

At soft peak, the peaks on the egg white will flop; at stiff peak, only the very tops will flop. Egg whites, when properly whisked, will triple in volume.

Index

Index

Index

Index

Photographers: Alan Benson, Cris Cordeiro, Craig Cranko, Ben Dearnley, Joe Filshie, Jared Fowler, Scott Hawkins, Ian Hofstetter, Chris L. Jones, Jason Lowe, Ashley Mackevicius, Andre Martin, Rob Reichenfeld, Brett Stevens.

Food Stylists: Kristen Anderson, Marie-Hélène Clauzon, Jane Collins, Carolyn Fienberg, Jane Hann, Mary Harris, Katy Holder, Cherise Koch, Sarah de Nardi, Michelle Noerianto, Sarah O'Brien, Sally Parker.

Food Preparation: Alison Adams, Shaun Arantz, Rekha Arnott, Jo Glynn, Sonia Grieg, Ross Dobson, Michelle Earle, Michelle Lawton, Michaela Le Compte, Valli Little, Olivia Lowndes, Kerrie Mullins, Briget Palmer, Kim Passenger, Justine Poole, Julie Ray, Christine Sheppard, Dimitra Stais, Angela Tregonning, and the Murdoch Books Test kitchen.

Laurel Glen Publishing
An imprint of the Advantage Publishers Group
5880 Oberlin Drive, San Diego, CA 92121-4794
www.laurelglenbooks.com

All notations of errors or omissions should be addressed to Laurel Glen Publishing, Editorial Department,
at the above address. All other correspondence (author inquiries, permissions, and rights) concerning the
content of this book should be addressed to Murdoch Books® a division of Murdoch Magazines Pty Ltd,
Pier 8/9, 23 Hickson Road, Millers Point NSW 2000, Australia.

NOTE: Those who might be at risk from the effects of salmonella poisoning (the elderly, pregnant women,
young children, and those with a compromised immune system) should consult their physician before
trying recipes made with raw eggs.

ISBN 1-59223-282-5
Library of Congress Cataloging-in-Publication Data available upon request.

Printed by Tien Wah Press, Singapore
1 2 3 4 5   08 07 06 05 04

Editorial Project Manager: Victoria Carey
Editor: Gordana Trifunovic
Designer: Michelle Cutler
Photographer (chapter openers): Jared Fowler
Stylist (chapter openers): Cherise Koch
Production: Fiona Byrne
Photo Library Manager: Anne Ferrier
Editorial Director: Diana Hill
Creative Director: Marylouise Brammer
Chief Executive: Juliet Rogers
Publisher: Kay Scarlett

You may find cooking times vary depending on the oven you are using. For convection ovens, as a
general rule, set the oven temperature 40°F lower than indicated in the recipe.

We have used large eggs in all recipes.